Great Women
of the Bible

Dorothee Soelle
Joe H. Kirchberger

Great Women of the Bible

IN ART AND LITERATURE

Foreword by Herbert Haag
Art Direction by Anne-Marie Schnieper

FORTRESS PRESS

Minneapolis

1

3

4

GREAT WOMEN OF THE BIBLE
In Art and Literature
Abridged edition, Fortress Press, 2006

Translated by Joe H. Kirchberger
from the German *Große Frauen der Bibel in Bild und Text,* published by Herder Verlag, Freiburg/Basel/Vienna, © 2001. All rights reserved.
Except for brief quotations in critical articles or reviews, no part of this book may be reproduced in any manner without prior written permission from the publisher.
Visit http://www.augsburgfortress.org/copyrights/contacts.asp or write to Permissions, Augsburg Fortress, Box 1209, Minneapolis, MN 55440.

9

A production of EMB-Service for Publishers Adligenswil/Lucerne
© 2001 EMB-Service for Publishers Adligenswil/Lucerne www.embservice.ch

ISBN 0-8006-3557-4

Printed in Italy

09 08 07 06 10 9 8 7 6 5 4 3 2 1

1 Lilith. *Persian amulet*
2 Eve. *Painting (detail) by Hans Memling*
3 Sarah and Hagar. *Rudolf von Ems, World Chronicle*
4 Tamar und Judah. *Painting (detail) by Jacopo Bassano*
5 Ruth. *Painting (detail) by Marc Chagall*
6 Abigail. *Painting (detail) by David Teniers d. Ältere*
7 Judith with the Head of Holofernes. *Painting (detail) by Jan Massys*
8 Queen Esther. *Painting (detail) by Andrea del Castagno*
9 The Anointing Woman. *Painting (detail) by Lucas Moser*
10 Mary and Martha. *Painting (deatil) by Jacob Jordaens*
11 Mary Magdalene. *Painting (detail) by The Master of Moulins*

Foreword

Herbert Haag

This book is about women but is not written for women only. It has taken almost two thousand years for the Christian world to discover the women of the Bible. Although the churches are committed to the Bible, the great diversity of female personalities in the Bible contributed only modestly to the Christian view of women. Women were, in fact, denied the liberty that certain biblical women themselves model (in spite of cultural limitations). The Age of Enlightenment and the French Revolution brought calls for equality and human rights for all, but only the feminist movement of our day accomplished an irrevocable commitment to such rights. Thus, in the plenary session of the Ecumenical Council, women came forward, asking for the ordination of women. And since the 1980s there have been first attempts to establish theology of women (and for women) as a regular teaching branch. Such theological research goes beyond theology per se and extends into analysis of culture and science. Women are no longer just the object, but also the instigators of research.

Feminist theology began with study and exegesis of the Bible. The masculine characterization of God was discussed, biblical language (brothers, sons) analyzed, and new avenues of symbolism explored. A universal anthropology became visible. In particular, suppressed and "forgotten" traditions of biblical women were brought to light.

Two biblical women have always been in vogue: Eve and Mary. Eve, as the mother of all life, but particularly as the seductress of man, Mary as the mother of Jesus who was ultimately removed from earthly reality and enthroned as the Queen of Heaven. In Mary woman's destination was outlined: she was to be likewise pure, sublime, and virginal. Eve, however, was thought to define woman's essential character—instinct-ridden, seductive, lacking in wisdom, evil, and dangerous for man.

Both Eve and Mary have been eminent sources of inspiration for art. Eve, to take one instance, is depicted on a bas-relief in Autun seduced by a serpent and changed into a serpent herself. It is thanks to this same Eve that woman, naked and dangerous, gained entrance into a church hostile to the body and sexual expression. And, among innumerable representations of Mary are those that offer to men, particularly to priests under a vow of celibacy, the opportunity to dedicate themselves and their sexuality to God's work.

Other women were also portrayed by artists, though always in terms of simple, black-and-white contrast: on the one hand, Delilah, Mary Magdalene, Bathsheba; on the other, Rebekah, Hannah, Elizabeth. Black or white: complex historical figures were not in demand.

Who were these biblical women really, and how did they live? It is often difficult, if not impossible, to learn this from the texts. After Israel had struggled through to the concept of a single God, understood by means of masculine images and terminology, woman was more and more devalued and reinterpreted by the biblical writers. Deborah, the great prophetess and judge, who by her courage and inspiration had united the tribes of Israel into a magnificent uprising against the Canaanite kings, falls into oblivion, whereas her fainthearted general Barak is praised two more times in the Bible. A similar case is that of Junia. In Romans 16:7 Paul salutes Andronicus and Junia, who had been apostles before him. Until the Middle Ages, theologians never doubted that Junia was a woman. But then, by Martin Luther and others, *Junia* was silently corrected to the masculine form *Junias*. An apostle could no longer be a woman.

Other women were forgotten altogether, such as the one who, in an hour of despair, anointed Jesus with precious spikenard. His disciples thought this gesture out of place and grumbled, whereupon Jesus rebuked them: "Wherever the good news is proclaimed in the whole world, what she has done will be told in remembrance of her" (Mark 14:3–9). But this prophecy did not come true, as we do not even know the name of the woman. (In John 12:3 she is identified as Lazarus's sister.)

When we proceed to the historic women, the Bible presents us with a whole gamut of characters. In the one-thousand-year history of Israel there is no episode where women have not played a decisive role, from Deborah around 1100 B.C. to Alexandra, queen of the Hasmoneans, and Salome, daughter of Herodias, who demanded the head of John the Baptist (Mark 6:25; Matthew 14:8). The latter demonstrates that women can also be cruel. Their rank, origin, and social standing also vary. Hagar

Eve: *painting by Albrecht Dürer (1471–1528), Medieval ideals of female beauty still prevail, but in this painting of Eve a new spirit is already noticeable: a more refined sensuality and a trace of decadence.*
Museo del Prado, Madrid

Marc Chagall

is a servant, Rahab an innkeeper and harlot. There is the necromancer of Endor, the queen of Sheba, and, once again, the judge and prophetess Deborah. True, there are also the two women fighting over a child who are, after all, only introduced to glorify the wisdom of Solomon. Still, it is remarkable how many of these women gave the history of Israel a decisive turn and a new face. Even though we cannot take as a historical fact the story of the "harlot" Rahab who hides Joshua's spies and helps them escape, the narrative demonstrates that a woman was thought to be capable of courage, cunning, and imagination. The fact that she was a whore did not bother storytellers of the Old Testament, and that she actually did not "belong" was rather in her favor, in the eyes of the early church. The same is true for Bathsheba, who was won by David through his adultery. The history of Israel would have run a different course had she not managed, before David's death, to make her son Solomon his successor on the throne.

Women may have their successes and triumphs, but in those days their lives were darkened by tragedy and suffering, even more than today. This was partly just human destiny, which ruled then as much as today. The beautiful, high-spirited Rachel, for whom Jacob gladly served for seven years (Gen. 29:20: "and they seemed to him but a few days because of the love he had for her") had to die when she gave birth to her second child by the wayside (Gen. 35:16 f.). Years of waiting and a short period of happiness were her destiny. And though Bathsheba was happy with David, she had to share him with half a dozen other women.

In all, the position of women in a patriarchal society was troublesome. So we should not be surprised when they resorted to cunning to have things their way. The conduct of Ruth, who crawls under Boaz's blanket while he, the man she wants, spends the night "at the end of the heap of grain" (Ruth 3:7), as the Bible reports with veiled frankness, does present a challenge even to our present concept of ethics. The Bible shows us women to whom a remark of Teilhard de Chardin applies: "To get ahead, one has to throw oneself forward, take a chance in trying everything. . . . One has to march alone, and frequently do something forbidden, suspicious."

Opposite: Boaz and Ruth, *painting by Marc Chagall (1887–1985). Boaz felt immediate affection for Ruth, whose modest demeanor had caught his attention as he observed the reaping. Boaz married Ruth, and she bore him a son named Obed.*
Musée National du message biblique, Nice.

The story of Abigail, too, contains an element of tragedy (1 Sam. 25). With disarming eloquence, the beautiful woman saves her nasty husband from David's revenge, and the king is so fascinated by her charm and cleverness that for her sake he not only pardons the avaricious and unjust Nabal, but after his death takes Abigail promptly into his house. Both seem to have found perfect happiness. Yet Abigail's name is mentioned only twice thereafter, and then we hear no more of her. She disappears in David's harem.

Looking at the fate of women in the Old Testament, we must conclude that though there are exceptions, they were typically disadvantaged, a fact that did not change much in the Christian era. There are many examples: according to Numbers 30, a husband may make void any vows he has given to his wife; in their partnership, he enjoys much more freedom than she. Legally, he may have several wives simultaneously and have relations with other women as long as they are not married. He may dismiss his wife quite unceremoniously. By the time of Jesus, these rules had led to so many abuses that he felt compelled to intervene. He wanted to spare them distress that God had never intended to impose upon women, and wanted to restore their dignity.

Still, a closer look shows how self-assured and independent the women of Israel could be. Beautiful Rebekah accepts from an utter stranger a golden nosering and two golden bracelets at the well. Later, by a neat trick, this same Rebekah procures the right of the firstborn for her favorite son, Jacob (Gen. 27). Again at a well, Rachel allows Jacob to kiss her, without knowing who he is, causing Jacob to cry with joy (Gen. 29:11).

If we discount the differences in social, cultural and religious conditions, the women of the Bible are like today's women, in their sorrow and joy, love and passion, freedom and dependence, their intelligence and resignation to their fate. But they were wrongly ignored for years by theologians and preachers. Women had to rediscover women. By digging into the biographies of these great women they have been able, also, to rediscover themselves in the Bible.

Eve and Lilith

Genesis
Chapter 1, verses 26–29; chapter 2, verses 1–25;
chapter 3, verses 1–24; chapter 4, verses 1–2

Above: Lilith, a winged Sumerian goddess, with angled raised arms, pointed head covering, and horned animals at her feet. Terracotta relief, symmetrically shaped, around 2000 B.C. Israel Museum, Jerusalem

Right: The large stone figure of shapely Eve is by Tilman Riemenschneider, between 1491 and 1493. This Eve is the counterpart of a figure of Adam at the portal of the Lady Chapel in Würzburg.

Opposite: To create Eve, God has come down to earth, causing Adam to fall into a deep sleep. Upon God's divine command, Adam's future companion is emerging from his rib, a new human being with a softly rounded body, a woman. Eve, not yet quite detached from Adam's side, raises her hands in gesture of supplication toward her Creator. Fresco from the ceiling of the Sistine Chapel, Rome, by Michelangelo (1475–1564).

The first chapter of the first book of the Old Testament (Genesis) recounts how God created the world in five days. He brought light into being, separated the water from the dry land, created plants and trees, sun, moon, and stars, and finally animals of all kinds. The text continues:

Then God said, "Let us make humankind in our image, according to our likeness; and let them have dominion over the fish of the sea, and over the birds of the air, and over the cattle, and over all the wild animals of the earth, and over every creeping thing that creeps upon the earth."

27 So God created humankind in his image, in the image of God he created them; male and female he created them.

28 God blessed them, and God said to them, "Be fruitful and multiply, and fill the earth and subdue it; and have dominion over the fish of the sea and over the birds of the air and over every living thing that moves upon the earth." 29 God said, "See, I have given you every plant yielding seed that is upon the face of all the earth, and every tree with seed in its fruit; you shall have them for food."

2 Thus the heavens and the earth were finished, and all their multitude. 2 And on the seventh day God finished the work that he had done, and he rested on the seventh day from all the work that he had done. 3 So God blessed the seventh day and hallowed it, because on it God rested from all the work that he had done in creation.

4 These are the generations of the heavens and the earth when they were created. In the day that the LORD God made the earth and the heavens, 5 when no plant of the field was yet in the earth and no herb of the field had yet sprung up—for the LORD God had not caused it to rain upon the earth, and there was no one to till the ground; 6 but a stream would rise from the earth, and

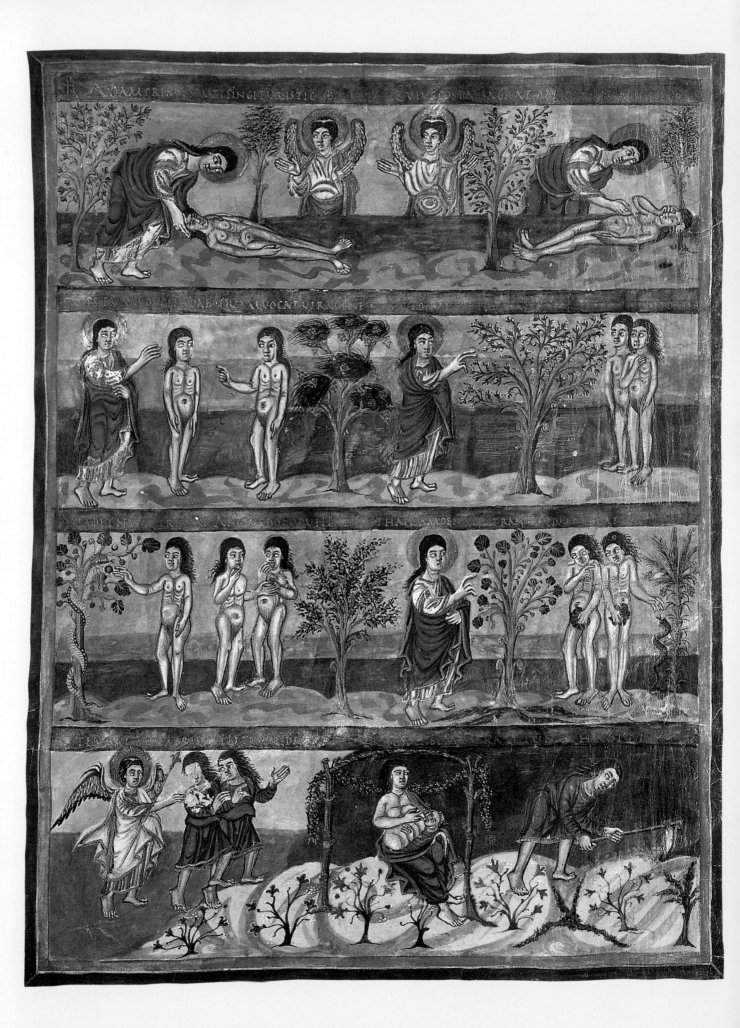

Opposite: The story of the creation of humanity up to the expulsion from Paradise is shown on four horizontal bands on a leaf of the Grandval-Bible, in Tours (ca. 840). In the upper row, angels look on as God forms the bodies of Adam and Eve.

In the second row, God blesses the human couple.

In the third, Eve succumbs to the temptation of the snake; Adam and Eve eat from the forbidden fruit and stand before God, conscious of guilt and ashamed of their nakedness.

On the bottom, they are driven away from Paradise by an archangel. Now Adam tills the soil "by the sweat of his face," while Eve nurses a child.
Add. Ms. 10546, fol. 5 v. British Library, London

O, she would have loved to stay

in this country for a while,

observing the animals' harmony and cleverness.

Rainer Maria Rilke

Above: The snake, hanging down from a branch, has persuaded Eve to pick an apple from the forbidden tree. She dangles this beautiful red fruit over Adam, who is sleeping peacefully, so that he may partake of it when he awakes. Painting by Beryl Cook, "in the naïve manner."

Left: Adam and Eve in Paradise, painting by Aloïs Beneš (1903–1985), Offenbach. The first human couple dwell in the Garden of Eden in perfect communion with nature. Bearded Adam is petting a bear, and a giant serpent nestles its head against Eve's leg. Trees supply fruit to eat, and flowers fill the air with sweet fragrance.
Fritz Novotny Collection, Offenbach

water the whole face of the ground —7 then the LORD God formed man from the dust of the ground, and breathed into his nostrils the breath of life; and the man became a living being. 8 And the LORD God planted a garden in Eden, in the east; and there he put the man whom he had formed. 9 Out of the ground the LORD God made to grow every tree that is pleasant to the sight and good for food, the tree of life also in the midst of the garden, and the tree of the knowledge of good and evil. 10 A river flows out of Eden to water the garden, and from there it divides and becomes four branches. 11 The name of the first is Pishon; it is the one that flows around the whole land of Havilah, where there is gold; 12 and the gold of that land is good; bdellium and onyx stone are there. 13 The name of the second river is Gihon; it is the one that flows around the whole land of Cush. 14 The name of the third river is Tigris, which flows east of Assyria. And the fourth river is the Euphrates. 15 The LORD God took the man and put him in the garden of Eden to till it and keep it. 16 And the LORD God commanded the man, "You may freely eat of every tree of the garden; 17 but of the tree of the knowledge of good and evil you shall not eat, for in the day that you eat of it you shall die."

18 Then the LORD God said, "It is not good that the man should be alone; I will make him a helper as his partner." 19 So out of the ground the LORD God formed every animal of the field and every bird of the air, and brought them to the man to see what he would call them; and whatever the man called every living creature, that was its name. 20 The man gave names to all cattle, and to the birds of the air, and to every animal of the field; but for the man there was not found a helper as his partner. 21 So the LORD God caused a deep sleep to fall upon the man, and he slept; then he took one of his ribs and closed up its place with flesh. 22 And the rib that the LORD God had taken from the man he made into a woman and brought her to the man. 23 Then the man said, "This at last is bone of my bones and flesh of my flesh; this one shall be called Woman, for out of Man this one was taken." 24 Therefore a man leaves his father and his mother and clings to his wife, and they become one flesh. 25 And the man and his wife were both naked, and were not ashamed.

3 Now the serpent was more crafty than any other wild animal that the LORD God had made. He said to the woman, "Did God say, 'You shall not eat from any tree in the garden'?" 2 The woman said to the serpent, "We may eat of the fruit of the trees in the garden; 3 but God said,

'You shall not eat of the fruit of the tree that is in the middle of the garden, nor shall you touch it, or you shall die.'" 4 But the serpent said to the woman, "You will not die; 5 for God knows that when you eat of it your eyes will be opened, and you will be like God, knowing good and evil." 6 So when the woman saw that the tree was good for food, and that it was a delight to the eyes, and that the tree was to be desired to make one wise, she took of its fruit and ate; and she also gave some to her husband, who was with her, and he ate. 7 Then the eyes of both were opened, and they knew that they were naked; and they sewed fig leaves together and made loincloths for themselves.

8 They heard the sound of the LORD God walking in the garden at the time of the evening breeze, and the man and his wife hid themselves from the presence of the LORD God among the trees of the garden. 9 But the LORD God called to the man, and said to him, "Where are you?" 10 He said, "I heard the sound of you in the garden, and I was afraid, because I was naked; and I hid myself." 11 He said, "Who told you that you were naked? Have you eaten from the tree of which I commanded you not to eat?" 12 The man said, "The woman whom you gave to be with me, she gave me fruit from the tree, and I ate." 13 Then the LORD God said to the woman, "What is this that you have done?" The woman said, "The serpent tricked me, and I ate." 14 The LORD God said to the serpent, "Because you have done this, cursed are you among all animals and among all wild creatures; upon your belly you shall go, and dust you shall eat all the days of your life. 15 I will put enmity between you and the woman, and between your offspring and hers; he will strike your head, and you will strike his heel." 16 To the woman he said, "I will greatly increase your pangs in childbearing; in pain you shall bring forth children, yet your desire shall be for your husband, and he shall rule over you." 17 And to the man he said, "Because you have listened to the voice of your wife, and have eaten of the tree about which I commanded you, 'You shall not eat of it: cursed is the ground because of you; in toil you shall eat of it all the days of your life; 18 thorns and thistles it shall bring forth for you; and you shall eat the plants of the field. 19 By the sweat of your face you shall eat bread until you return to the ground, for out of it you were taken; you are dust, and to dust you shall return."

20 The man named his wife Eve, because she was the mother of all living. 21 And the LORD God made garments of skins for the man and for his

wife, and clothed them. ²² Then the LORD God said, "See, the man has become like one of us, knowing good and evil; and now, he might reach out his hand and take also from the tree of life, and eat, and live forever"—²³ therefore the LORD God sent him forth from the garden of Eden, to till the ground from which he was taken. ²⁴ He drove out the man; and at the east of the garden of Eden he placed the cherubim, and a sword flaming and turning to guard the way to the tree of life.

4 Now the man knew his wife Eve, and she conceived and bore Cain, saying, "I have produced a man with the help of the LORD." ² Next she bore his brother Abel. Now Abel was a keeper of sheep, and Cain a tiller of the ground.

The Original Sin, *painting by the Venetian master Tintoretto (Jacopo Robusti) (1518–1594). Eve is characterized as the more active partner in the temptation scene. From her elevated position, she leans toward Adam, her body bathed in bright, warm light. The expression of her face is tender but also slightly melancholy as she offers the forbidden fruit to the recoiling Adam. Accademia Venezia, Venice*

Eve and Lilith | 15

Left: Detail from the panel painting on wood in tempera by the Sienese master Giovanni di Paolo (1400–1482). The pale blue background against which the fruit-laden trees and meadow flowers are set off conveys the idyllic beauty of the Garden of Eden. The angel who urges Adam and Eve to leave seems well disposed toward the couple and ready to give them a piece of advice to take along.
Metropolitan Museum, New York

Above: Hand in hand Adam and Eve leave the garden of Paradise, adorned with flowers and golden trees, from which the angel has expelled them. They have covered their nakedness with dense leaves. The snake, crawling behind them, carries a figleaf. This seventeenth-century piece comes from the Topkapi-Serail Museum in Istanbul.

Eve and Lilith | 17

The mother of all living

Dorothee Soelle

Eve is the "mother of all living." Her name is traced back to the word for "life"; it may be older than the biblical narrative. "Mother of all living" is a title frequently employed in the Near East for the first woman; the Sumerians called her "Inanna," the Babylonians "Tiamat," and in Egypt she was worshiped as "Isis." Eve is strong and beautiful, and Adam greets her with exuberant joy: she creates life. Even after the murder of Abel she does not want to be separated from her son Cain. She represents the life-affirming principle.

God created two beings, male and female, who together form God's image. His essence can only be expressed in two different beings. Difference, disparity, and polarity between the sexes were there from the beginning, not the androgynism assumed by some cultures. The first report of the creation celebrates the duality of humanity.

In Genesis 2 and 3, written by a different author, the story of "the beginning" is related differently: God shapes and breathes rather than creating by his mere word; woman is derived from man, made from his rib, as if the statement of their equal origin —"male and female he created them"—were no longer valid. In this second version, it is the woman who desires knowledge instead of remaining in the innocence of Paradise. Eve, who, like the animals, gets her name from Adam, is the driving force behind change.

The creation narrative has a slight flavor of antifeminism, which only later, in the patriarchal exegesis, becomes the main theme. There is a tradition of denigrating women that is more pronounced in the history of Christianity than in Jewish writing. Its most important symbols are the rib and the apple. These were used to explain woman's physical, intellectual, and moral inferiority. Women are only a part, never the whole; the "second sex," not the first, therefore "after and below man," as even the eminent twentieth-century theologian Karl Barth has expressed it. Adam talks; Eve is silent and finds her joy in him. She achieves her identity from and through the man. In many cultures to this day, a woman who marries must adopt the man's name and has no name of her own.

Eve is regarded as inferior not only because she was created later, and from Adam's rib, but also because she allied herself with the snake, ate from the tree of knowledge, and was thus responsible for the expulsion from Paradise. In this part of the Genesis account, Eve is no longer man's silent partner and object of his admiration; by contrast, she takes matters into her own hands. She acts, she converses with the serpent (to the chagrin of all male theologians), and from this discussion she attains new insight: she learns that humans do not in fact die by acquiring knowledge.

In her unabashed curiosity she discovers that which alters the course of human life. "The woman saw that the tree was good for food, and that it was a delight to the eyes, and to be desired to make one wise. . . ." Eating, aesthetics, and knowledge (both intellectual and sexual) belong together. It is only after the couple have tasted the fruit that their eyes are opened.

For Friedrich Schiller, the "fall" from grace was the happiest moment of history. In the biblical text, the words "sin" and "fall" do not appear, but "expel" does occur. Expulsion is one phase of giving birth: the fetus expelled from the mother's body where all that is necessary for life has been provided. It is after the expulsion that life begins— work, exertion and sexuality.

In leaving the garden, Adam and Eve confront the coldness and harshness of life. They discover themselves, experience the joy of learning and the happiness of beauty and knowledge. Without Eve, we all would still be sitting under trees, innocently dreaming. Instead, we have eaten from the tree of knowledge, without having attained the tree of life. The biblical myth illustrates this by means of the curses falling upon the first couple. Herein lies the explanation for why life is so painful and troublesome: curse, enmity, suffering, domination, sadness, sweat—these are the essential words used in the Bible. Adam is punished because he followed Eve's initiative. Eve is punished doubly, both by her labor and pain in giving birth and by her submission to the man.

Work and sexuality, the predominant expressions of life for the mature individual, are described as a curse. In a biblical tradition that is preoccupied with repressing elements, these curses have been promoted to an inevitable fate; as if thistles in the field, pain at childbirth, and submission of one part of mankind to another were necessary and unchangeable. However, they are not part of the "order of creation" imposed by the punishing God, but rather the contrary: these curses demonstrate their distance from the good creation and describe realistically the farmer's life in Palestine. "In the beginning" there was no hostility between nature and man and no senseless drudgery of work without happiness. Eve and Adam were to "cultivate and preserve" the garden; together they were to be the icons of God, without resorting to domination, suppression, and force. Eve was conceived at the creation as the mother of all living, not the "vessel of sin" that the church fathers made her to be.

Christianity brings Eve and Mary together, one being complemented by the other. The injustice done to Eve it has tried to compensate through Mary. Some women bear the name of "Eva-Marie," possibly to remind us that the desire to learn and the wish to be an independent human being do not destroy the capacity to transcend the self. We do not have to choose between Mary, the gentle maiden, and Eve, the woman who refuses to accept any limits. We are able to include characteristics of both women in our consciousness.

The original title of this painting by George Frederick Watts (1817–1904) was She Shall Be Called Woman. *The reference is to Eve, the ancestress, here presented by the artist with golden hair, surrounded by flowers and beautifully plumed birds, as the source of all joys in life. Watts himself remarked, "In her lofty majesty of innocence, Eve represents the prototype of all that all of mankind may hope for." Tate Gallery, London*

The thoughtless, fleeting enjoyment of that apple

has caused the world's unending misery.

Goethe, *Natürliche Tochter*

Above: The snake, with a crowned woman's head, has enticed Adam and Eve to taste the fruit from the tree of knowledge. Detail of an illustration from the Bible Commentary (ca. 1459–1462) by Nicholas of Lyra.

Left: Painting by Hans Memling (1433–1494). Kunsthistorisches Museum, Vienne

Opposite: Adam and Eve by Tintoretto (1518–1594). Eve's beautiful body is in mellow light, and Adam's back is turned away from the viewer. Adam leans forward to grasp (or possibly to reject?) the proffered fruit, and Eve is the one recoiling.
Scuola di San Rocco, Venice

Ceiling painting in the Sistine Chapel by Michelangelo (1475–1564), showing the Fall from Grace and the Expulsion from Paradise. To the left of the tree of knowledge, Adam, far from being seduced by Eve to taste the forbidden fruit, reaches eagerly into the fig tree. Eve, reclining, reaches toward the snake, endowed with the body of a woman, who places a fig into her outstretched hand. To the right of the tree of knowledge the couple is shown being driven from Paradise by an angel bearing a sword.

Ancient and medieval sources

Joe H. Kirchberger

Eve, the progenitor of humanity, has been shrouded in legendary lore since the pre-Christian era. In Jewish literature she is not typically the centerpiece of the legends but is always mentioned in connection with other figures—above all, with Adam, but also with the snake (often identified with Satan) and with mysterious Lilith, supposedly Adam's first wife.

IN JEWISH LEGEND, Adam is the ideal man, for whom the world was created. He was formed by God's own hands, not, like all other creatures, by his word. His body is said to mirror the whole world: his hair is like the forest, his tears like a river, his mouth like the ocean, and as the ocean surrounds the earth, so the white of his eyes surrounds the iris. God took dust from all four corners of the world to create Adam. Therefore, when he dies he will return to the earth from whence he came. Only a few of his exceptional qualities are inherited by his offspring: Samson has his strength, Absalom his hair, Saul his neck—and these very qualities bring disaster to those who possess them.

He is earthly, for he eats, drinks, excretes his waste, and procreates like the animals. But he is also angelic, for he can speak, think, walk upright, and look toward heaven. The angels of love are said to have advocated his creation, but the angels of truth advised against it, for he would be full of lies and quarrelsome. God destroyed those opposing angels, except their leaders Michael and Gabriel. A third group, led by Labbiel, gave in to the angels of love, and therefore God changed the name of Labbiel to Raphael, meaning "God rescues."

Satan, the tallest and most beautiful angel—he had twelve wings, the other angels only six—was jealous of Adam, but since he could not call the animals by their correct names, as Adam could, God flung him down to earth. Since that time, there has been enmity between him and humanity.

When the other angels saw Adam, they were ready to worship him, until God put him to sleep and they saw that he was a mere mortal. First God gave him Lilith to be his wife—this is the way the story in the first chapter of Genesis was interpreted. She was made of dust like Adam and therefore considered herself of equal rank. But Adam presumed to be her master since he had been created first. There was a quarrel, and Lilith promptly vanished. When Adam complained, God sent three angels to fetch her. They finally found Lilith in the Red Sea, but she refused to return. For this God punished her with the loss of one hundred of her demon children every day. Lilith is said in the legends to avenge herself on children (although they can protect themselves with an amulet showing the names of the three angels sent to fetch her) and to seduce men with her beautiful hair.

THE FIGURE OF LILITH dates to Babylonian-Assyrian and possibly even older Sumerian sources. Not until the Talmud, which was written between the second and fifth century A.D., is she identified as Adam's first wife.

The Bible itself mentions her but once, in Isaiah 34:14, as one of the creatures who inhabits the devastated land of Edom. Luther translates inexactly with "kobold" (sprite), the King James translation calls her a "screech-owl," and a more recent American translation has "night-monster." The Talmud makes her Adam's first wife as a means of accounting for the disparity between the two Genesis accounts of the creation of the first humans. In the first chapter, man and woman are created by God simultaneously and in the same manner, while in the second, Adam is created at first alone; then Eve is formed from his rib, so that he may have a companion.

According to Jewish tradition, Eve ranks below Adam, for she was made from his body: not from his head lest she should be proud, not from his eye lest she should look around lecherously, not from his ear lest she should eavesdrop, not from his mouth lest she become a chatterbox, and not from his foot lest she should wander away, but from a chaste part of his body. And in forming her, God said to each part: "Be chaste, be chaste!" Yet in spite of these precautions, woman has obtained many qualities God did not wish her to have: many a woman is proud, Sarah was an eavesdropper, Rachel envied Leah, and Eve herself reached for the forbidden fruit.

If God had not made Adam fall asleep, he could not have loved Eve: men do not love women they have known since their youth. But when Adam woke up and saw Eve, he said: "It is she who

Not from his head
lest she should be proud,
not from his eye lest she
should look around
lecherously,
not from his ear lest she
should eavesdrop,
not from his mouth lest
she become a chatterbox,
and not from his foot
lest she wander away,
but from a chaste part
of his body.

From a Jewish legend

This painting, entitled Eve
Tempted, *belongs to George
Frederick Watts's (1817–1904)
Eve trilogy, which ends with
Eve repenting. Here, Watts
shows Eve, a leopard at her feet,
becoming intoxicated with the
scent of a blossoming bush. She
turns her head upward as the
snake speaks to her, captivated
by its enticing words.*
Tate Gallery, London

makes my heart throb in the night." Because the woman was made from man's flesh, she needs perfume, as meat requires salt to be preserved. On the other hand, woman is not as easily pacified as man, for a few drops of water suffice to soften up earth while a bone immersed in water will remain hard for many days.

Eve called Adam her lord and master. Their wedding was celebrated with unequaled pageantry. God himself led Eve to dance with Adam, adorned her, and blessed the couple while the angels danced. Adam called her Ishash, and himself Ish. And the angels brought them food and drink.

No sooner had Eve eaten the forbidden fruit— not identified as an apple in the Bible—than she saw the angel of death before her and expected her end. She persuaded Adam to taste the fruit too because she feared that he would take another woman after her death. Then she gave the fruit to all the animals and made them mortal in this way. Only the bird Malham refused and therefore lives forever in Paradise.

In the beginning, both Adam's and Eve's bodies were covered by a thick skin. This now dropped off, and the radiance that had surrounded them disappeared. And as they were ashamed of their nakedness, they sought to cover it with branches, but all trees denied them their branches, except the fig tree—for the forbidden fruit had been a fig.

The angels expected the first couple to die after the Fall, but God explained to them: "I have said they would die on the day they tasted the forbidden fruit. But I had the kind of day in mind which lasts a thousand years." This is why in the first generations same people lived to be nine hundred and older, but no one surpassed a thousand years.

When after the Fall God called Adam to account, he blamed Eve. The legends say that both were punished only because they did not confess their guilt; otherwise God would have forgiven them. The snake, however, was punished without a trial: its hands and feet were hacked off so that ever after it had to crawl on its belly. For God knew that it had seduced Eve only to bring about Adam's death: the snake itself wanted to marry Eve after Adam was out of the way. The earth, too, was punished, as God made it dependent on rain. And finally, the moon was punished for having laughed when all the angels and the sun wept over the punishment of Adam and Eve. Her light was reduced and she was made to wane and disappear every month before she could renew herself.

After their expulsion Adam and Eve built a hut and sat in it, crying and sobbing for seven days. Then they went out searching for food but found none. At that point they repented: Adam made Eve stand in the Tigris River, and he himself stood in the Jordan River. But after eighteen days Satan persuaded Eve to give up her repentance and confessed that he had brought about her fall because he was jealous of Adam.

When Adam was 930 years old, he fell sick, and Eve, in tears, begged him to transfer half of his sickness onto her. Then she and her third son, Seth, wandered to the gates of Paradise and requested from God the oil of mercy but were refused. God promised them, however, that in the future this oil would be granted to the God-fearing—but only to them—after their resurrection.

When Adam died Eve cried and begged God not to separate her from Adam's body from which she bad come. God heard her and let her die too, six days after Adam. An archangel descended and advised Seth on how to bury Eve. Before her death Eve advised her children to record on stone the story of the first humans.

ALL THESE ADORNMENTS of the biblical text go back to pre-Christian Jewish literature. The Jewish Book of Adam of this period was translated into many Near Eastern languages and further embellished. In some of these versions, the original Adam is said to have been gigantic, reaching from earth into the sky, with a huge head. Only after the Fall did he shrink in size. Generally, the history of mankind after Adam and Eve is presented as a decline. According to the Jewish Midrash, Adam originally had a tail; God took it from him to honor him. He was also considered to be a magician and is said to have procured a horoscope at the birth of Noah. Jewish legend ascribes to him a Book of the Times, a Book of Astronomy, and other writings which he bequeathed to his son Seth. According to a later Jewish legend, Adam and Eve were transferred to the moon after their deaths. Even nowadays all newborn boys cry "A" for Adam when they are born, while the girls cry "E" for Eve.

Opposite: The English painter Dante Gabriel Rossetti (1828–1882) painted many portraits of women whom he endowed with a mystic-sensuous quality, in memory of the beloved wife he had lost after only two years of marriage. The painting, entitled Lady Lilith, showing a woman with magnificent hair, is a new interpretation of prebiblical Lilith. For Rossetti, Lilith is not an evil demon, but essential woman, combining worldly and divine love.
Metropolitan Museum, New York

Mephistopheles to Faust in the "Walpurgis Night" scene:

"'Tis the first wife of the first man. Adam's first wife, Lilith. Beware, beware of her bright hair. . . .

Many a young man she beguileth, smiles winningly on youthful faces,

But woe to him whom she embraces!"

Goethe, *Faust I*

Above: Jacopo Bassano (1510–1592), a master of the Venetian late Renaissance, was noted for his genre scenes of peasants. Here Adam and Eve are shown as a peasant couple, settled and content in their humble life. Only the skull at the lower right recalls the Fall by which they have forfeited immortality. Galleria Palatina, Florenz

Opposite: Half-length portrait of Eve by Duncan Grant (1885–1978). This archaistic presentation dates to 1913, a period in which the artist was experimenting with a combination of medieval and ultramodern styles. The overlong neck is reminiscent of Modigliani, while Eve's head with its huge eyes staring straight at the viewer and the raised arms suggest painted icons. Eve's only garment, a veil hanging from the forehead down the back, recalls Picasso's Nude with Veil, *which Grant declared to be his favorite Picasso painting. In spite of this mixture of styles, Duncan Grant has created a magnificent, convincing portrait of Eve. Tate Gallery, London*

In the Talmud, one can also find the notion that Adam was androgynous, with two faces, until he was sawed apart by God. A similar idea can be found in other cultures and is mentioned in Plato's Symposium. Adam is sometimes said to have stayed away from his wife after the Fall for 130 years. To repent, he did not remove his belt of figleaves during this time. From his tears of repentance the rivers Euphrates and Tigris originated, while those of Eve were turned into pearls.

CHRISTIAN LEGENDS of the early Middle Ages also show contradictory tendencies. On the one hand, Eve, the sinner who caused mankind's misery, is disparaged: she is said to have been made from a dog—or a monkey tail—even in as late a poem as that of Hans Sachs (1557). On the other hand, the story of the Fall is tied more and more directly to that of redemption through Christ. This connection is made as early as the so-called Ezzolied, written

Eve: But if one of us must go first,
it is my prayer that it shall be I;
for he is strong, I am weak,
I am not so necessary to him as
he to me—life without him would
not be life; how could I endure it?
This prayer is also immortal, and
will not cease from being offered
up while my face continues.
I am the first wife; and in the last wife
I shall be repeated.
Adam: (at Eve's grave): Wheresoever
she was, there was Eden.

Mark Twain, *Eve's Diary*

around 1065 by a Bamberg priest. In the popular *Legenda Aurea* (Golden Legend) of Jacobus de Voragine, archbishop of Genoa (around 1290), which greatly influenced medieval literature, as well as in Heinrich von Freiberg's *Legend of the Holy Cross* and in *Kreuzleich* of the minnesinger Frauenlob (Heinrich von Meissen), the wood of Christ's cross is said to have come from the tree of knowledge. Adam becomes Jesus' counterpart, and Eve Mary's. These contrasting ideas show up particularly clearly in the Anglo-Norman Jeu d'Adam of the twelfth century, where Adam and Abel announce the coming of the Redeemer, but in the end are dragged to hell by devils. According to the Golden Legend, the fall from grace took place on a Friday at the sixth hour, which is also the hour of Christ's crucifixion. These connections between the Fall and the history of redemption have the effect of diminishing somewhat Adam and Eve's

culpability; responsibility for mankind's misery is attributed to the devil instead.

In the Koran, the sacred book of Islam, compiled shortly after the death of its founder (632 A.D.), the story of Paradise is briefly narrated in the second surah. But Eve is hardly mentioned. God (Allah) teaches Adam the names of the animals and commands the angels to kneel before Adam. They all do it, except for Iblis—a name probably corrupted from Diabolus, "devil"—who is an infidel. And it is Iblis, Satan, who expels the couple from Paradise.

Sarah and Hagar

Genesis
Chapter 12, verses 1–3, 10–20;
Chapter 15, verses 1–5; Chapter 16, verses 1–16 :
Chapter 17, verses 15–22; Chapter 18, verses 1–16;
Chapter 20, verses 1–18; Chapter 21, verses 1–21;
Chapter 23, verses 1–20

*The actual history of the people of Israel begins
with Abraham, originally Abram. As explained
in the eleventh chapter of the first book of Moses
(Genesis), he was a descendant of Shem in the
seventh generation, and a son of Terah. His
brothers were named Nahor and Haran. Lot,
son of Haran and Abram's nephew, became his
companion when both, upon God's command,
left Ur in Chaldea and journeyed to Canaan.*

*Opposite: Through his customs officials at the
border, the Egyptian pharaoh has learned of Sarai's
beauty and had her brought before his throne. She
is standing behind her husband Abram, who pre-
tends to be her brother, fearing he will be killed
if he is known to be her husband; one could then
dispose of her at will. As her "brother," Abram
is treated courteously and even given presents by
Pharaoh. Detail from the* Octateuch, Byzantine,
twelfth century, tempera on parchment.
Biblioteca Apostolica Vaticana, Vatican

Now the LORD said to Abram, "Go from your country and your kindred and your father's house to the land that I will show you. 2 I will make of you a great nation, and I will bless you, and make your name great, so that you will be a blessing. 3 I will bless those who bless you, and the one who curses you I will curse; and in you all the families of the earth shall be blessed." 10 Now there was a famine in the land. So Abram went down to Egypt to reside there as an alien, for the famine was severe in the land. 11 When he was about to enter Egypt, he said to his wife Sarai, "I know well that you are a woman beautiful in appearance; 12 and when the Egyptians see you, they will say, 'This is his wife' then they will kill me, but they will let you live. 13 Say you are my sister, so that it may go well with me because of you, and that my life may be spared on your account." 14 When Abram entered Egypt the Egyptians saw that the woman was very beautiful. 15 When the officials of Pharaoh saw her, they praised her to Pharaoh. And the woman was taken into Pharaoh's house. 16 And for her sake he dealt well with Abram; and he had sheep, oxen, male donkeys, male and female slaves, female donkeys, and camels. 17 But the LORD afflicted Pharaoh and his house with great plagues because of Sarai, Abram's wife. 18 So Pharaoh called Abram, and said, "What is this you have done to me? Why did you not tell me that she was your wife? 19 Why did you say, 'She is my sister' so that I took her for my wife? Now then, here is your wife, take her, and be gone." 20 And Pharaoh gave his men orders concerning him; and they set him on the way, with his wife and all that he had.

15 After these things the word of the LORD came to Abram in a vision, "Do not be afraid, Abram, I am your shield; your reward shall be very great." 2 But Abram said, "O LORD God, what will you give me, for I continue childless, and the heir of my house is Eliezer of Damascus?" 3 And Abram said, "You have given me no offspring, and so a slave born in my house is to be my heir." 4 But the word of the LORD came to him, "This man shall not be your heir; no one but your very own issue shall be your heir." 5 He brought him outside and said, "Look toward heaven and count the stars, if you are able to count them." Then he said to him, "So shall your descendants be."

16 Now Sarai, Abram's wife, bore him no children. She had an Egyptian slave-girl whose name was Hagar, 2 and Sarai said to Abram, "You see that the LORD has prevented me from bearing children; go in to my slave-girl; it may be that I shall obtain children by her." And Abram listened to the voice of Sarai. 3 So, after Abram had lived

ten years in the land of Canaan, Sarai, Abram's wife, took Hagar the Egyptian, her slave-girl, and gave her to her husband Abram as a wife. [4] He went in to Hagar, and she conceived; and when she saw that she had conceived, she looked with contempt on her mistress. [5] Then Sarai said to Abram, "May the wrong done to me be on you! I gave my slave-girl to your embrace, and when she saw that she had conceived, she looked on me with contempt. May the LORD judge between you and me!" [6] But Abram said to Sarai, "Your slave-girl is in your power; do to her as you please." Then Sarai dealt harshly with her and she ran away from her. [7] The angel of the LORD found her by a spring of water in the wilderness, the spring on the way to Shur. [8] And he said, "Hagar, slave-girl of Sarai, where have you come from and where are you going?" She said, "I am running away from my mistress Sarai." [9] The

angel of the LORD said to her, "Return to your mistress, and submit to her." [10] The angel of the LORD also said to her, "I will so greatly multiply your offspring that they cannot be counted for multitude." [11] And the angel of the LORD said to her, "Now you have conceived and shall bear a son; you shall call him Ishmael, for the LORD has given heed to your affliction. [12] He shall be a wild ass of a man, with his hand against everyone, and everyone's hand against him; and he shall live at odds with all his kin." [13] So she named the LORD who spoke to her, "You are El-roi"; for she said, "Have I really seen God and remained alive after seeing him?" [14] Therefore the well was called Beer-lahai-roi; it lies between Kadesh and Bered. [15] Hagar bore Abram a son; and Abram named his son, whom Hagar bore, Ishmael. [16] Abram was eighty-six years old when Hagar bore him Ishmael.

17 ⁱ⁵ God said to Abraham, "As for Sarah your wife, you shall not call her Sarai, but Sarah shall be her name. ¹⁶ I will bless her, and moreover I will give you a son by her. I will bless her, and she shall give rise to nations; kings of peoples shall come from her." ¹⁷ Then Abraham fell on his face and laughed, and said to himself, "Can a child be born to a man who is a hundred years old? Can Sarah, who is ninety years old, bear a child?" ¹⁸ And Abraham said to God, "O that Ishmael might live in your sight!" ¹⁹ God said, "No, but your wife Sarah shall bear you a son, and you shall name him Isaac. I will establish my covenant with him as an everlasting covenant for his off-spring after him. ²⁰ As for Ishmael, I have heard you; I will bless him and make him fruitful and exceedingly numerous; he shall be the father of twelve princes, and I will make him a great nation. ²¹ But my covenant I will establish with Isaac, whom Sarah shall bear to you at this season next year." ²² And when he had finished talking with him, God went up from Abraham.

18 The Lᴏʀᴅ appeared to Abraham by the oaks of Mamre, as he sat at the entrance of his tent in the heat of the day. ² He looked up and saw three men standing near him. When he saw them, he ran from the tent entrance to meet them, and bowed down to the ground. ³ He said, "My Lᴏʀᴅ, if I find favor with you, do not pass by your servant. ⁴ Let a little water be brought, and wash your feet, and rest yourselves under the tree. ⁵ Let me bring a little bread, that you may refresh yourselves, and after that you may pass on—since you have come to your servant." So they said, "Do as you have said." ⁶ And Abraham hastened into the tent to Sarah, and said, "Make ready quickly three measures of choice flour, knead it, and make cakes." ⁷ Abraham ran to the herd, and took a calf, tender and good, and gave it to the servant, who hastened to prepare it. ⁸ Then he took curds and milk and the calf that he had prepared, and set it before them; and he stood by them under the tree while they ate. ⁹ They said to him, "Where is your wife Sarah?" And he said, "There, in the tent." ¹⁰ Then one said, "I will surely return to you in due season, and your wife Sarah shall have a son." And Sarah was listening at the tent entrance behind him. ¹¹ Now Abraham and Sarah were old, advanced in age; it had ceased to be with Sarah after the manner of women. ¹² So Sarah laughed to herself, saying, " After I have grown old, and my husband is old, shall I have pleasure?" ¹³ The Lᴏʀᴅ said to Abraham, "Why did Sarah laugh, and say, 'Shall I indeed bear a child, now that I am old?' ¹⁴ Is anything too wonderful for the Lᴏʀᴅ? At the set time

Above: Illustration from the Queen Mary Psalter, *early fourteenth century. On top: God's promise to Abraham: "I will make you exceedingly fruitful; and I will make nations of you, and kings shall come from you. . . ." Below: Abraham informs Sarah of God's promise.* British Library, London

Opposite: Hagar's Return, *painting by Pietro Berretini da Cortona (1596–1669). An angel has appeared to the desperate Hagar, who fled into the desert to escape harsh treatment by her mistress Sarah. The angel insists that she return, and Abraham welcomes her with open arms. Although he tolerated Sarah's earlier rulings, he deeply regrets his wife's severity toward Hagar.* Kunsthistorisches Museum, Vienna

Sarah and Hagar | 33

OX ETTRIF ORMIS ANGELORC TRINITAS
Senif renifit hofpıtıf mappalıa
Etıam quıctam farrae malıuum ferulc

The Lord appeared to Abraham by the oaks of Mamre, as he sat at the entrance of his tent in the heat of the day. He looked up and saw three men standing near him.

Genesis 18:1–2

Above: **Abraham and the Three Angels,** Prudentius-handschrift, *Carolingian, second half of the twelfth century. Abraham steps in front of his tent and invites the angels to rest with him. Burgerbibliothek, Bern*

Opposite: This mosaic of the fifth century, Abraham Entertaining the Three Angels, *is one of the thirty-five mosaics above the epistyle of Santa Maria Maggiore in Rome. Abram, left front, orders his wife Sarai to prepare the meal. At right, behind the table, are angels to whom Abram then serves the dishes.*

I will return to you, in due season, and Sarah shall have a son." 15 But Sarah denied, saying, "I did not laugh"; for she was afraid. He said, "Oh yes, you did laugh." 16 Then the men set out from there, and they looked toward Sodom; and Abraham went with them to set them on their way.

20 From there Abraham journeyed toward the region of the Negeb, and settled between Kadesh and Shur. While residing in Gerar as an alien, 2 Abraham said of his wife Sarah, "She is my sister." And King Abimelech of Gerar sent and took Sarah. 3 But God came to Abimelech in a dream by night, and said to him, "You are about to die because of the woman whom you have taken; for she is a married woman." 4 Now Abimelech had not approached her; so he said, "LORD, will you destroy an innocent people? 5 Did he not himself say to me, 'She is my sister'? And she herself said, 'He is my brother.' I did this in the integrity of my heart and the innocence of my hands." 6 Then God said to him in the dream, "Yes, I know that you did this in the integrity of your heart; furthermore it was I who kept you from sinning against me. Therefore I did not let you touch her. 7 Now then, return the man's wife; for he is a prophet, and he will pray for you and you shall live. But if you do not restore her, know that you shall surely die, you and all that are yours."

8 So Abimelech rose early in the morning, and called all his servants and told them all these things; and the men were very much afraid. 9 Then Abimelech called Abraham, and said to him, "What have you done to us? How have I sinned against you, that you have brought such great guilt on me and my kingdom? You have done things to me that ought not to be done." 10 And Abimelech said to Abraham, "What were you thinking of, that you did this thing?" 11 Abraham said, "I did it because I thought, there is no fear of God at all in this place, and they will kill me because of my wife. 12 Besides, she is indeed my sister, the daughter of my father but not the daughter of my mother; and she became my wife. 13 And when God caused me to wander from my father's house, I said to her, 'This is the kindness you must do me: at every place to which we come, say of me, He is my brother'"

14 Then Abimelech took sheep and oxen, and male and female slaves, and gave them to Abraham, and restored his wife Sarah to him. 15 Abimelech said, "My land is before you; settle where it pleases you." 16 To Sarah he said, "Look, I have given your brother a thousand pieces of silver; it is your exoneration before all who are with you; you are

completely vindicated." 17 Then Abraham prayed to God; and God healed Abimelech, and also healed his wife and female slaves so that they bore children. 18 For the LORD had closed fast all the wombs of the house of Abimelech because of Sarah, Abraham's wife.

21 The LORD dealt with Sarah as he had said, and the LORD did for Sarah as he had promised. 2 Sarah conceived and bore Abraham, a son in his old age, at the time of which God had spoken to him. 3 Abraham gave the name Isaac to his son whom Sarah bore him. 4 And Abraham circumcised his son Isaac when he was eight days old, as God had commanded him. 5 Abraham was a hundred years old when his son Isaac was born to him. 6 Now Sarah said, "God has brought laughter for me; everyone who hears will laugh with me." 7 And she said, "Who would ever have said to Abraham that Sarah would nurse children? Yet I have borne him a son in his old age."

8 The child grew, and was weaned; and Abraham made a great feast on the day that Isaac was weaned. 9 But Sarah saw the son of Hagar the Egyptian, whom she had borne to Abraham, playing with her son Isaac. 10 So she said to Abraham, "Cast out this slave woman with her son; for the son of this slave woman shall not inherit along with my son Isaac." 11 The matter was very distressing to Abraham on account of his son. 12 But God said to Abraham, "Do not be distressed because of the boy and because of your slave woman; whatever Sarah says to you, do as she tells you, for it is through Isaac that offspring shall be named for you. 13 As for the son of the slave woman, I will make a nation of him also, because he is your offspring." 14 So Abraham rose early in the morning, and took bread and a skin of water, and gave it to Hagar, putting it on her shoulder, along with the child, and sent her away. And she departed, and wandered about in the wilderness of Beer-sheba.

15 When the water in the skin was gone, she cast the child under one of the bushes. 16 Then she went and sat down opposite him a good way off, about the distance of a bowshot; for she said, "Do not let me look on the death of the child." And as she sat opposite him, she lifted up her voice and wept. 17 And God heard the voice of the boy; and the angel of God called to Hagar from heaven, and said to her, "What troubles you, Hagar? Do not be afraid; for God has heard the voice of the boy where he is. 18 Come, lift up the boy and hold him fast with your hand, for I will make a great nation of him." 19 Then God opened her eyes and she saw a well of water. She went, and filled the skin with water, and gave the boy a drink.

Abimelech said, "My land is before you; settle where it pleases you."

To Sarah he said, "Look, I have given your brother a thousand pieces of silver; it is your exoneration before all who are with you; you are completely vindicated."

Genesis 20:15–16

King Abimelech returns to Abraham his wife Sarah. Gobelin tapestry of the seventeenth century in the cathedral of Freiburg im Breisgau. While living as a stranger in Gerar, Abraham introduced Sarah as his sister, as he had done once before in Egypt. King Abimelech had heard of Sarah's beauty and had her brought before him. But God revealed to him in a dream that Sarah was a married woman and that he would die if he kept her with him. The king, deeply shocked, summoned Abraham the following day to return to him Sarah whom he had not touched.

20 God was with the boy, and he grew up; he lived in the wilderness, and became an expert with the bow. 21 He lived in the wilderness of Paran; and his mother got a wife for him from the land of Egypt.

23 Sarah lived one hundred twenty-seven years; this was the length of Sarah's life. 2 And Sarah died at Kiriath-arba (that is, Hebron) in the land of Canaan; and Abraham went in to mourn for Sarah and to weep for her.

12 Then Abraham bowed down before the people of the land. 13 He said to Ephron in the hearing of the people of the land, "If you only will listen to me! I will give the price of the field; accept it from me, so that I may bury my dead there." 14 Ephron answered Abraham, 15 "My LORD, listen to me; a piece of land worth four hundred shekels of silver —what is that between you and me? Bury your dead." 16 Abraham agreed with Ephron; and Abraham weighed out for Ephron the silver that he had named in the hearing of the Hittites, four hundred shekels of silver, according to the weights current among the merchants.

17 So the field of Ephron in Machpelah, which was to the east of Mamre, the field with the cave that was in it and all the trees that were in the field, throughout its whole area, passed 18 to Abraham as a possession in the presence of the Hittites, in the presence of all who went in at the gate of his city. 19 After this, Abraham buried Sarah his wife in the cave of the field of Machpelah facing Mamre (that is, Hebron) in the land of Canaan. 20 The field and the cave that is in it passed from the Hittites into Abraham's possession as a burying place.

Hagar and the Angel, *Giovanni Benedetto Castiglione (1616–1670) shows, in a Rembrandtesque chiaroscuro, Hagar kneeling on the ground with an empty water jug. Her feverish son has drunk all the water and is dying of thirst. But in a bright cloud, an angel appears, pointing a well out to Hagar and telling her to take good care of Ishmael as his and her fortunes are closely connected. This is the first hint that Hagar, through Ishmael, will become the ancestress of many Arab peoples.*
Palazzo Rosso, Genoa

The laughter of the mistress, the misery of the slave

Dorothee Soelle

The Scriptures speak not only of patriarchs, but also of "matriarchs" such as Sarah and Hagar. Both women have their share of faith, but even more of doubt; both are part of the promise, though indirectly and in no way triumphantly. As mothers of sons, both are implicated to this day in the tragic conflicts of the Middle East between Jews, the children of Isaac, and Arabs, the children of Ishmael.

Sarah is the extremely beautiful wife of a prosperous shepherd. Twice her husband presents her as his sister to protect himself against assaults. Is he some kind of a procurer who profits from his wife's beauty? In the beginning Sarah appears as the silent pawn while Abraham acts and God saves. What she thinks or feels is not mentioned. Only her laughter is remembered when the three angels announce a son to her, the ironic laughter of an aging postmenopausal woman who hears everything that is important (Gen. 18:12). This laughter is the first real sign of life from Sarah in the biblical narrative. Afraid, she then tries to disavow her laughter but God speaks to her directly, not via Abraham, and changes her bitter laughter into laughter of unexpected happiness (Gen. 21:6–7).

The bitter years of childlessness have hardened Sarah. She tries a borrowed motherhood, using an Egyptian slave named Hagar. Abraham now stands between women—one married, wealthy, and free but old and childless; the other unmarried, poor, and dependent but young and fertile. Sarah, once in Egypt the object of men's intrigues, is now active in handling the powerless black slave girl. Abraham, wishing to avoid a conflict, leaves pregnant Hagar to Sarah's mercy. For her, Hagar is but a tool not a person; she never mentions her name nor addresses her subordinate. Sarah is in full control of the situation; she tells Abraham what to do, and he appears as a quiet, compliant secondary figure in the drama of the two women.

With her pregnancy Hagar is changing. The barriers of rank and hierarchy fall away: she looks down upon her mistress, an old, childless woman. Her pride is awakened, but she is humiliated at once. "And Sarah dealt harshly with her" (Gen.

16:6); the same expression is used for the subjugation of the Israelites in Egypt. In this story of two women, Sarah is now playing the part of Pharaoh's overseers, as we can imagine them from reports of the slave age: more work, less food; no free time, humiliations and chastisements . . .

Pregnant Hagar runs away from the house of slavery into the desert. She has had to sell her body all her life—not just in servitude, but now also in maternal surrogacy. She flees through the arid desert to the Egyptian border: "The angel of the Lord found her" (Gen. 16:7); God's messenger follows and talks to her. The black slave girl is the first person in the Bible to be visited by God's messenger. His command is harsh, but in keeping with her chances of survival, Hagar is to return into slavery and misery. "Return to your mistress, and submit to her" (Gen. 16:9), the angel says to her. He then promises her what is typically only promised to fathers: numerous offspring and the blessed name of her still unborn child, Ishmael, "for the Lord has given heed to your affliction." God has heard her misery, even when she was not crying. And he has secured her future: her son who will grow up in the desert. Suffering and hope combine, and Hagar calls the stranger who met her in the desert by a new name. "Thou God seest me" (Gen. 16:13 KJV). She returns strengthened and remains under God's protection even when she is sent into the desert a second time and must watch her child dying of thirst. This time she has no choice; she is exiled. When the water she had taken along has come to an end, she steps aside, saying, "'Do not let me look on the death of the child.' And as she sat opposite him, she lifted up her voice and wept" (Gen. 21:16). God hears her and opens her eyes to see a well of water nearby. An angel rescues Ishmael, father of the Arab peoples, from death in a waterless country.

During the last ten years, Hagar's story has been read time and again by women living in misery. While they reflect on their situation, they remember the pregnant, humiliated, exiled woman of the Bible. In Brazil I met a group of black domestics who, for a miserable wage under slavelike conditions, work from morning till night. They wash,

clean, iron, and mind the children of the rich while their own children have to find a way to survive in the slums. The exploitation does not spare their bodies: many, for fear of losing their jobs, submit to abuse and rape by their masters and their sons. When they become pregnant, they are sent into the desert, like Hagar. Young girls are sold to middlemen for about a thousand dollars and then offered to tourists at the airports. This, too, is a kind of desert.

Hagar's story is an inspiration and encouragement for today's impoverished, struggling women. As God helped Hagar to lead a free and dignified life, so he will liberate us. They pray together, as they have learned from the black slave girl: "Thou God seest me. . . ."

Sarah, shown here as a stooped and aged woman, complains to Abraham of Hagar's defiant attitude since she became pregnant. Abraham tries to avoid involvement by saying it is up to Sarah how to deal with her slave. Pen-and-ink drawing by Rembrandt (1606–1669), around 1640.
Musée du Louvre, Paris

Ancient and medieval sources

Joe H. Kirchberger

Jewish legend has greatly embellished the saga of Abram's journey. According to some sources, it is only when the patriarch comes to Egypt that he realizes how beautiful his wife Sarai is (whose name, like Abram's own, was changed by God at a later date). To conceal her from the Egyptians, Abram hides her in a box, and when the customs officials at the border inquire about its contents, he answers "barley." "No," they say, "it is wheat." "All right," says Abram, "I shall pay the higher toll for wheat." But then they charge that the box contains pepper, then gold, and finally precious stones, and Abram gives in every time. This behavior only arouses suspicion, and Abram is forced to open the box. When the officials discover Sarai's beauty, they immediately send messengers to Pharaoh, who rewards them richly and dispatches an army to lead Sarai to his palace.

Abram and Sarai, now separated, both pray to God for help. As Sarai stands before Pharaoh, an angel appears to her—but only she can see him. He consoles her and announces that God has heard both their prayers. When Pharaoh asks her about Abram, she refers to him as her brother. Pharaoh then sends a quantity of silver, pearls, sheep, and oxen to Abram and sets up a marriage contract according to which Sarai will inherit all his gold and silver, his slaves, and the province of Goshen. He even surrenders his own daughter Hagar to be Sarai's slave.

At night, however, when he tries to approach Sarai, the angel appears, and when Pharaoh is about to remove her shoe, he is struck on the hand with a rod. When he touches Sarai's dress, he is struck again. The angel asks Sarai if he should continue, and she implores him to grant Pharaoh a little respite. But Pharaoh and his entire court are struck with leprosy, and when he consults his priests, they explain to him the reason for his affliction: his intention to marry Sarai. Upon hearing this he returns the untouched Sarai to Abram.

Later, when Sarai sends Hagar in to Abram, she feels no jealousy, for Hagar, is her property, not Abram's. In ancient Israel there was, it seems, an ancient custom of childless women having their slave girls beget children for them. One encounters the same situation when Leah and Rachel offer their slaves to Jacob, who then bear him sons.

Hagar shows her arrogance, according to Jewish legend, when the pregnant girl tells visitors: "My mistress Sarai is not what she seems to be. She cannot be as righteous and God-fearing as she appears, for otherwise how could she be childless after so many years, while I am already carrying Abram's child?" When Abram turns Hagar over to Sarai for punishment, she not only treats Hagar as a lowly slave, but casts her the "evil eye." Hagar, in contrast to what the biblical text says, loses her child and then runs away. The angels who persuade her to return promise her that she will be pregnant again and give birth to Ishmael—Ishmael being the first of six children on whom God bestowed a name before they were born (the others being Isaac, Moses, Solomon, John the Baptist, and the Messiah).

When God appears to him in the plains of Mamre (Gen. 18:1), Abram's name has already been changed by God: not Abram ("the father is great") but Abraham ("father of a multitude") was to be his name from now on. Sarai's change in name is equally significant, for "Sarah" means princess.

Jewish sources also dispute the apparent identification in the biblical text of the three men who with God himself visit Abraham after his circumcision. The three are, rather, the archangels Michael, Gabriel, and Raphael. Raphael has come to heal Abraham's wound; Michael, to convey the good news to Sarah; and Gabriel, to carry out Sodom and Gomorrah's destruction. On the other hand, it is a Jewish tradition that Sarah was the only woman to whom God talked directly, as he had not done to Eve.

IN ANOTHER EPISODE preceding Isaac's birth, the Bible records how Sarah was coveted by the King of Gerar, and again Abraham calls her his sister; the earlier episode with Pharaoh is repeated

Opposite: Hagar's Expulsion *by Nicolaes Maes (1634–1693), a painter of the Dutch baroque period. Abraham is shown as a patriarch with flowing beard, wide gown, and Near Eastern head covering, radiating dignity and commanding respect.*
Alte Pinakothek, Munich

in almost every detail. But Jewish legend adds one variant: King Abimelech gives Sarah a long, precious gown that covers her charms—a silent reproach to Abraham, who has carelessly exposed his wife to the lecherous eyes of strangers.

When Isaac is finally born, so say the legends, God also remembers all other childless women and allows them to bear children. When Isaac grows up, there is trouble between him and Ishmael. Ishmael, nicknamed the "scoffer" and the "wild one," demands two-thirds of Abraham's inheritance, leaving only one-third to Isaac. He also threatens Isaac with his bow and arrow—only in jest, he claims. These incidents prompt Sarah's resentment and her casting an evil eye upon Ishmael when he and Hagar are sent into the desert. Ishmael becomes so ill that Hagar has to carry her grown-up son. Because he is feverish, she uses up all the water she had taken along, which otherwise would have been sufficient for both. Hagar searches for the same willow bushes where once before the angels had found her. There Ishmael, now God-fearing, asks God for help, and God causes water to gush up from Miriam's spring, which he had created on the sixth day of creation. Hagar is able to fill up her water bottle and return to Egypt with Ishmael.

THE STORY OF Isaac's sacrifice, too, has been embellished by Jewish legend: first Satan appears to young Isaac in the guise of a very old man and whispers to him that God wants to sacrifice him. But Abraham recognizes Satan and sends him away. He then goes to Sarah and gives her the same story. Sarah trembles and almost dies with grief, but then stands erect and says, "Whatever God has commanded Abraham to do, may he do it in peace!" Later Satan lies to Sarah, saying Isaac has indeed been sacrificed. She cries and mourns her son and sets out to find him until Satan relents and tells her the truth: Isaac is alive. Overcome with sheer joy about this news, Sarah collapses and dies. Abraham and Isaac search for her and find her dead at Hebron. She still possesses the beauty and innocence of her youth.

After Sarah's death, misfortune overtakes the whole country, and Abraham, himself in mourning and in want of comfort, has nevertheless to console the inhabitants. He ages suddenly after Sarah's demise, but God's blessing remains with him: Hagar gives birth to a daughter, and Ishmael, regretting his former impetuosity, subordinates himself to Isaac. Only one thing is missing: a wife for Isaac.

HELLENISTIC PHILOSOPHY also dealt with the Sarah-Hagar story and interpreted it in various

Above: Hagar and Ishmael in the Desert, *painting by Jean-Charles Cazin (1841–1901). Ishmael clings to his mother Hagar, who cries desperately. The angel who will assist them and show them a well has not yet appeared. Cazin painted many landscapes with fine, tender atmospheres in which the human figures—often biblical as in this case—play a secondary role.*
Musée des Beaux Arts, Tours

Opposite: The Angel Appears to Hagar and Ishmael, *painting by Giovanni Battisto Tiepolo (1696–1770), one of the best-known of the Venetion painters of the eighteenth century.*
Scuola di San Rocco, Venice

Sarah said to Abraham, "Cast out this slave woman with her son ; for the son of this slave woman shall not inherit along with my son Isaac."
Genesis 21:10

God called to Hagar from heaven, and said to her, "What troubles you, Hagar? Do not be afraid; for God has heard the voice of the boy where he is.
Genesis 21:17–18

Above: Illustration from the World Chronicle *of Rudolf von Ems, written in the first half of the thirteenth century. The top panel shows Sarah expelling her servant Hagar and her little son Ishmael. In the lower panel, an angel appears to Hagar in the desert, showing her the way to a water well, so that she and her child may survive.*
Kantonsbibliothek (Vadiana) St. Galle, Ms 302 Vad.

Opposite: Sarah's Burial, *pen-and-ink drawing by Friedrich Preller the Elder 1804–1878, around 1874. A group of people in neoclassical style is set in a romantic forest landscape. Sarah is being buried in a rock tomb. Abraham had purchased a family vault from the Hittites so that Sarah could rest on home ground although she had died in a foreign country.*

ways. The Jewish philosopher Philo (Philo Judaeus) of Alexandria, who died around 50 A.D. and who attempted to reconcile the Hebrew Scriptures with Greek philosophy, saw in Hagar's subordination to Sarah a symbol for the humane disciplines: astronomy, rhetoric, music and grammar. Sarah for him represented wisdom and virtue; the particular disciplines are but the preliminary stages through which man has to pass before attaining this higher wisdom. The harsh treatment Hagar receives from Sarah is therefore not the result of jealousy but is caused by the higher judgment of those who have embraced the wisdom of the true philosopher.

THE APOSTLE PAUL also sees the story as an allegory, not, of course, in Philo's Neoplatonic sense, but as a Christian. In Galatians 4:21 he relates Hagar and Ishmael to the old covenant concluded on Mount Sinai. But Christians are descendants of Sarah, the free woman, as symbolized in the new covenant.

By contrast, Flavius Josephus, a Jewish historian of the first century A.D., gives us a purely human

explanation of the biblical story. He sees Abraham as a good man who grieves at his wife's childlessness, and Sarah as a good wife who brings her maidservant to him to please him. Hagar grows impertinent, but after her return mends her ways; she has to be expelled only because of her son's rivalry with Isaac. Even then Abraham hesitates and, out of the goodness of his heart, refuses for a long time to send her into the desert. Josephus endeavors to temper the cruel story of the expulsion and to show all concerned in their best possible light. Most Jewish interpreters of the Middle Ages follow the same trend, with the single exception of Nachmanides, around 1250, who declares Sarah and Abraham to be sinners and sees their punishment in the fact that the descendants of Ishmael have always harassed those of Sarah. Hagar's pride and independence are usually explained with reference to her being Pharaoh's daughter—a supposition not mentioned in the Bible.

IN THE LEGENDS OF Islam, Abraham and Ishmael are said to be the founders of the Kaaba, the holy shrine in Mecca. Sarah is denigrated; she and Isaac play secondary roles. When Hagar and Ishmael are sent into the desert toward Mecca, Allah causes the spring to gush forth; when Arab desert tribes see birds fly in this direction, they know that there must be water. Following them, they discover Hagar and give her some milk while she lets them drink the water. According to other Islamic legends, Abraham himself brings Hagar and Ishmael to Mecca. In any case, Ishmael is said to be the ancestor of the twelve tribes of North Arabia.

After Sarah's death and funeral, described in detail in the Bible, Abraham marries a second time. The Bible calls this new spouse Keturah (Gen. 25:1), but according to the Jewish biblical interpreter Rashi (around 1100) and others, Keturah and Hagar are one and the same, for "Keturah" means incense, and Hagar was called by that name after she had given up her idolatry, so that her deeds became as fragrant as frankincense.

Tamar

CUNNING VERSUS POWER

Genesis
Chapter 38, verses 1–30

The story of Tamar is of great importance for Israel's line of succession. This fact, however, becomes evident only in chapter 49 when Jacob, on his deathbed, blesses his sons but excludes Reuben from his birthright as firstborn because of his sin with Bilhah, and also his next-born sons, Simeon and Levi, because of their crimes at Shechem. It is thus his fourth son Judah who receives the coveted blessing. Tamar, who in the following chapters inserts herself into the line of succession by an extremely bold maneuver, apparently had foreseen that, for it is her son from Judah who stands in direct line to David and Solomon.

Opposite: Judah's Daughter-in-Law Tamar, *as painted by Marc Chagall (1887–1985) in 1960. Having been married to two of Judah's sons, both of whom died young and left her childless, Tamar was intent on having a son from her father-in-law. Disguised as a whore with her face hidden under a veil, she sat down on the road outside the gate where Judah had to pass by. He approached her and, not recognizing her as Tamar, said to the supposed whore: "Come, let me come into you." Afterward she demanded three objects from Judah as a pledge for a kid he had promised her. With these she would later prove that it was Judah who made her pregnant.*

Musée national du message biblique, Nizza

It happened at that time that Judah went down from his brothers and settled near a certain Adullamite whose name was Hirah. ² There Judah saw the daughter of a certain Canaanite whose name was Shua; he married her and went in to her. ³ She conceived and bore a son; and he named him Er. ⁴ Again she conceived and bore a son whom she named Onan. ⁵ Yet again she bore a son, and she named him Shelah. She was in Chezib when she bore him. ⁶ Judah took a wife for Er his firstborn; her name was Tamar. ⁷ But Er, Judah's firstborn, was wicked in the sight of the LORD, and the LORD put him to death, ⁸ Then Judah said to Onan, "Go in to your brother's wife and perform the duty of a brother-in-law to her; raise up offspring for your brother." ⁹ But since Onan knew that the offspring would not be his, he spilled his semen on the ground whenever he went in to his brother's wife, so that he would not give offspring to his brother. ¹⁰ What he did was displeasing in the sight of the LORD, and he put him to death also. ¹¹ Then Judah said to his daughter-in-law Tamar, "Remain a widow in your father's house until my son Shelah grows up"—for he feared that he too would die, like his brothers. So Tamar went to live in her father's house.

¹² In course of time the wife of Judah, Shua's daughter, died; when Judah's time of mourning was over, he went up to Timnah to his sheepshearers, he and his friend Hirah the Adullamite. ¹³ When Tamar was told, "Your father-in-law is going up to Timnah to shear his sheep," ¹⁴ she put off her widow's garments, put on a veil, wrapped herself up, and sat down at the entrance to Enaim, which is on the road to Timnah. She saw that Shelah was grown up, yet she had not been given to him in marriage. ¹⁵ When Judah saw her, he thought her to be a prostitute, for she had covered her face. ¹⁶ He went over to her at the road side, and said, "Come, let me come in to you," for he did not know that she was his daughter-in-law. She said, "What will you give me, that you may come in to me?" ¹⁷ He answered, "I will send you a kid from the flock." And she said, "Only if you give me a pledge, until you send it." ¹⁸ He said, "What pledge shall I give you?" She replied, "Your signet and your cord, and the staff that is in your hand." So he gave them to her, and went in to her, and she conceived by him. ¹⁹ Then she got up and went away, and taking off her veil she put on the garments of her widowhood.

²⁰ When Judah sent the kid by his friend the Adullamite, to recover the pledge from the woman, he could not find her. ²¹ He asked the townspeople, "Where is the temple prostitute who was at Enaim

Marc Chagall

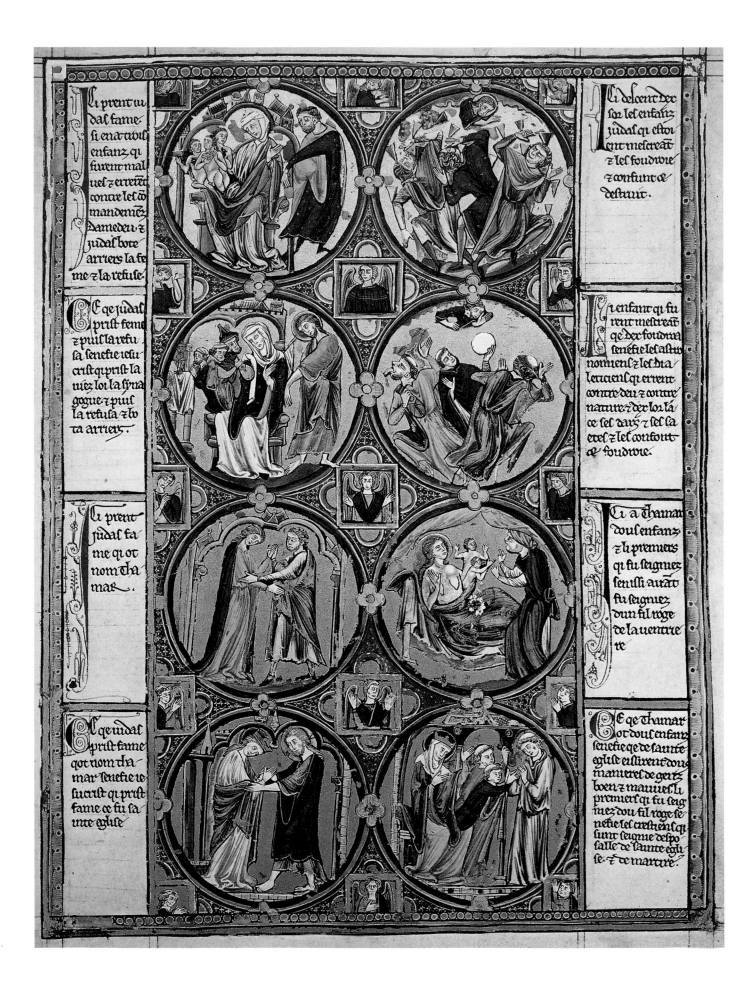

by the wayside?" But they said, "No prostitute has been here." 22 So he returned to Judah, and said, "I have not found her; moreover the townspeople said, 'No prostitute has been here.'" 23 Judah replied, "Let her keep the things as her own, otherwise we will be laughed at; you see, I sent this kid, and you could not find her."

24 About three months later Judah was told, "Your daughter-in-law Tamar has played the whore; moreover she is pregnant as a result of whoredom." And Judah said, "Bring her out, and let her be burned." 25 As she was being brought out, she sent word to her father-in-law, "It was the owner of these who made me pregnant." And she said, "Take note, please, whose these are, the signet and the cord and the staff." 26 Then Judah acknowledged them and said, "She is more in the right than I, since I did not give her to my son Shelah." And he did not lie with her again.

27 When the time of her delivery came, there were twins in her womb 28 While she was in labor, one put out a hand; and the midwife took and bound on his hand a crimson thread, saying, "This one came out first." 29 But just then he drew back his hand, and out came his brother; and she said, "What a breach you have made for yourself!" Therefore he was named Perez. 30 Afterward his brother came out with the crimson thread on his hand; and he was named Zerah.

She put off her widow's garments, put on a veil, wrapped herself up, and sat down at the entrance to Enaim, which is on the road to Timnah. . . . When Judah saw her, he thought her to be a prostitute, for she had covered her face. He went over to her at the road side, and said, "Come, let me come in to you," for he did not know that she was his daughter-in-law. . . .

Genesis 38:14–16

Opposite: Bible Moralisée *of the* Codex Vindobonensis *(early thirteenth century) 2554, fol. 8. Oesterreichische Nationalbibliothek, Vienna*

Right: Judah and Tamar, *painting by Jacopo Bassano (1515–1592). After Judah had slept with a supposedly unknown girl (who turned out to be Tamar) he promised her a kid from the flock, and as a pledge she demanded his signet and bracelets—signs of his judical office—and his shepherd's staff.*
Europart, Abbaye St. Martin de Ligugé

A woman infiltrates the power structure

Dorothee Soelle

Tamar is a Canaanite woman from Israel's early days. Judah, one of Jacob's twelve sons, has picked her to marry his oldest son. He has three sons and does not have to worry about his offspring; his name and possessions can be passed on and God will keep his promise. But Er, the oldest son, dies without children, so Judah sends his second son, Onan, to Tamar to provide descendants for his dead brother. This is in accordance with the old customs by which it is the duty of a brother to marry his sister-in-law if his brother died childless, so that the dead man does not lose his right to have descendants. Onan, Judah's second son, refuses to cooperate, apparently not by engaging in what has been named after him but by practicing coitus interruptus (Gen. 38:9). This displeases God, who lets him die. Now only Judah's third son is left, but he is withheld from Tamar under a pretext. Worse, Judah, the patriarch controlling all family matters, returns her as a childless widow to her father's house. Apparently Judah is apprehensive for his third son, fearing this ominous woman who has been the ruin of two men.

Tamar is only the object of all these intrigues by default, yet she must possess sufficient power to make her father-in-law want to get rid of her. Legally and socially, the situation of a childless and therefore useless widow sent back to her original owner, her father, is the very worst imaginable for a woman.

Tamar does not accept this state of affairs, however, but acts and helps herself in a most unusual manner for which she is neither criticized nor morally condemned by either the Bible nor by ancient Jewish tradition. She disguises herself as a whore and lies in wait for her traveling father-in-law. He sleeps with her without recognizing her. They agree on a kid from his flock as the reward for her favors.

In this story there is a clash of the older religion of the original Canaanites, dominated by fertility gods, and the rules of sexual behavior of the Israelites, regulated by marriage and inheritance laws. Among the Canaanite women there was a custom to consecrate a kid to Astarte, the goddess of love, whenever a woman gave herself to a stranger by the wayside. In Tamar's story these cultures merge and the fertility cult is integrated into the other religion of the god from the desert. The alien element, intercourse by the wayside and the sacrifice to the ancient goddess of love and fertility, is integrated with Judah's tribal policies. The alien woman who uses the traditions of her own people cunningly is not rejected, expelled, or condemned but recognized and honored as the ancestress of the tribe of Judah.

Tamar becomes pregnant and dresses again in her widow's clothing. She is taking a great risk, for officially she is still engaged to Shelah, Judah's third son, and adultery is punishable by burning or stoning. But she has taken precautions, demanding from Judah, instead of the promised kid, three pledges that identify him as a wealthy Jew. When he wants to redeem his pawns through a friend, the prostitute he had met has disappeared. No one knows her. Tamar had returned home immediately after their meeting.

When she is found to be pregnant, Judah orders her to be burned. Without any interrogation, she is dragged to the place of execution. But she sends up the signet, the bracelets, and the staff with a message to her father-in-law: "It is the owner of these who has made me pregnant" (Gen. 38:25). Thus her clever precaution exposes the truth. Tamar's deliberate and well-planned action refutes one of the oldest misogynistic myths, the belief that woman is brainless and driven by her desires. The pretended seductress turns out to be God's tool in his plan of salvation, even when behaving deceitfully. It is no accident that Judah, recognizing his paternity, uses the word "righteous" (Gen. 38:26) that was elsewhere applied to Abraham (Gen. 15:6). "She hath been more righteous than I" (KJV).

Thus Tamar infiltrates the mighty family structure that holds out no hope for her. She does not surrender herself to the silence of those condemned to powerlessness. Judah, Leah's fourth son, appears in this episode as the personification of a given legal, religious, and social power that time and again deprives women of any participation in power. The patriarchal structure, one of the curses pronounced at the expulsion from Paradise ("Your desire shall be for your husband, and he shall rule over you" [Gen. 3:16]) is not part of the good order

He went over to her at the road side, and said, "Come, let me come in to you," for he did not know that she was his daughter-in-law. She said, "What will you give me, that you may come in to me?" He answered, "I will send you a kid from the flock." And she said, "Only if you give me a pledge, until you send it." He said, "What pledge shall I give you?" She replied, "Your signet and your cord, and the staff that is in your hand." So he gave them to her, and went in to her, and she conceived by him.

Genesis 38:16–18

of creation, but evidence of decline after the Fall. It is not intended to remain forever, for patriarchal power has its limits. Tamar and other "strong women" of the Bible declare an entirely different history. God does not identify with the powerful men of this world. When Tamar fights against the injustice done to her with craftiness and perseverance, she is blessed with two sons by the God who has sanctioned irrevocably the strength of the weak, the stratagems of the disadvantaged, and the power of the powerless.

Tamar and Judah, *painting by Horace Vernet (1789–1863). Tamar had lost two husbands, both sons of Judah. Now, as Judah has refused to give her his third, youngest son, she has decided to seduce her father-in-law.*

Ancient and medieval sources

Joe H. Kirchberger

Tamar's story has been typically embellished by Jewish exegesis and legend.

Of Tamar's first husband, Er, it is said only that he was "wicked in the sight of the LORD." But according to the legends, he committed the same sins as his successor and brother, Onan, whose name lives on in the English and German languages. Of Tamar herself it is said that she was Shem's daughter, or the daughter of Shem's son Aram.

The name "Er" means "the childless one." Er's mother, Bath-Shuah, is said to have plotted against her non-Canaanite daughter-in-law so that Er stayed away from her. Only three days after their marriage, an angel is said to have killed him. Onan married Tamar even before the funeral rites for Er had come to an end! He then lived with Tamar for one year. His mother kept on plotting, but Judah threatened Onan, who then agreed to sleep with Tamar, but without begetting a child. "Onan" means "grief." After he, too, had died, say the legends, Judah intended to give Tamar to his youngest son, Shelah, who was still a child. But Bath-Shuah would not permit this because she hated Tamar, and when Judah was absent one day, she brought in a Canaanite wife for Shelah. This action enraged Judah and led to Bath-Shuah's own death. Now Judah wanted to wait until Shelah had grown up, but Tamar had prophetic gifts and knew that she was to be the ancestress of David and the Messiah; therefore she decided to act at once.

Judah had never seen her face since Tamar had always modestly veiled her face. That is why he did not recognize her when she offered herself to him. She was rewarded for this modesty by becoming not only the ancestress of David, but also of the prophets Isaiah and Amos.

When they met on the way to Timnah, Judah, it is said, first passed her without paying attention, but she prayed and an angel forced Judah to return to her. The pledges she demanded from him, signet, bracelet, and staff, are the emblems of royalty, judiciary office, and of the Messiah; they symbolize their mutual descendants.

WHEN TAMAR WAS on trial, Isaac, Jacob and Judah are said to have been her judges (according to the Bible, Isaac had already died by this time).

As the youngest of the judges, Judah pronounced his verdict first: Tamar, daughter of the high priest Shem, was to be burned as a whore. The other two assented. When Tamar attempted to justify herself and looked for her pawns, she could not find them because Sammael, the evil angel, had hidden them. She then prayed and promised God that if he would save her from being burned, her children would not fear death by fire for his glory. Now God sent the archangel Michael—or Gabriel—and he helped her to find the pawns. When Judah saw them, he is supposed to have been so stunned that he confessed not only his responsibility for Tamar's pregnancy but also the fact that he had, years earlier, helped to deceive his father when he and his brothers had faked Joseph's death. Reuben, too, confessed his guilt of having sinned with Bilhah. Thereupon Judah declared Tamar's innocence. But when he blamed himself for having delayed Tamar's marriage to Shelah too long, a voice from above sounded: "Both of you are innocent! This happened because it was God's will!"

Perez and Serach, the twins Tamar gave birth to, were as brave and devoted as their father, Judah. Legend has it that they were the two spies Joshua later sent to Jericho who were helped by Rahab. The thread mentioned in the Bible in connection with the twins' birth (Gen. 38:28–30) was the same thread Rahab then bound in the window as a sign for Joshua's army (Joshua 2:18).

In the poetic section of the Talmud, the Aggada, Judah is scarcely blamed for his sin with Tamar; rather, he is praised for his honesty and gallantry during her trial. Tamar, too, is largely exonerated for having acted like a whore. Philo says, for instance, that she grew up in a house of idolaters but was converted to Jewish faith, and that as a reward for the pure life she led, her descendants were honored like the true heirs of Jacob.

The rather complex family relations that resulted from Tamar's initiative soon became the subject of riddles.

Judah and Tamar, *painting by Jacopo Bassano (1515–1592). After Judah had slept with a supposedly unknown girl (who turned out to be Tamar) he promised her a kid from the flock, and as a pledge she demanded his signet and bracelets— signs of his judical office—and his shepherd's staff. Musée Fabre, Montpellier*

Ruth

The Moabite

*The book of Ruth, inserted in the Bible between
the book of Judges and the two books of Samuel,
does not report great political or religious events.
It is a kind of an idyll in the form of a short story.
The story of Ruth and Boaz clearly takes place
toward the end of the era of judges, for it is said
that her son Obed was the grandfather of David,
and Jewish legends claim that Ruth in her advanced
age still lived to see King Solomon in his glory.*

*Opposite: After Ruth had been gleaning all day,
Boaz still filled a piece of cloth with six measures
of barley. Add. MS 22413, fol. 71r (1315–1320).
British Library, London*

1 In the days when the judges ruled, there was a famine in the land, and a certain man of Bethlehem in Judah went to live in the country of Moab, he and his wife and two sons. 2 The name of the man was Elimelech and the name of his wife Naomi, and the names of his two sons were Mahlon and Chilion; they were Ephrathites from Bethlehem in Judah. They went into the country of Moab and remained there. 3 But Elimelech, the husband of Naomi, died, and she was left with her two sons. 4 These took Moabite wives; the name of the one was Orpah and the name of the other Ruth. When they had lived there about ten years, 5 both Mahlon and Chilion also died, so that the woman was left without her two sons and her husband.

6 Then she started to return with her daughters-in-law from the country of Moab, for she had heard in the country of Moab that the LORD had considered his people and given them food. 7 So she set out from the place where she had been living, she and her two daughters-in-law, and they went on their way to go back to the land of Judah. 8 But Naomi said to her two daughters-in-law, "Go back each of you to your mother's house. May the LORD deal kindly with you, as you have dealt with the dead and with me. 9 The LORD grant that you may find security, each of you in the house of your husband." Then she kissed them, and they wept aloud. 10 They said to her, "No, we will return with you to your people." 11 But Naomi said, "Turn back, my daughters, why will you go with me? Do I still have sons in my womb that they may become your husbands? 12 Turn back, my daughters, go your way, for I am too old to have a husband. Even if I thought there was hope for me, even if I should have a husband tonight and bear sons, 13 would you then wait until they were grown? Would you then refrain from marrying? No, my daughters, it has been far more bitter for me than for you, because the hand of the LORD has turned against me." 14 Then they wept aloud again. Orpah kissed her mother-in-law, but Ruth clung to her.

15 So she said, "See, your sister-in-law has gone back to her people and to her gods; return after your sister-in-law." 16 But Ruth said, "Do not press me to leave you or to turn back from following you! Where you go, I will go; where you lodge, I will lodge; your people shall be my people, and your God my God. 17 Where you die, I will die—there will I be buried. May the LORD do thus and so to me, and more as well, if even death parts me from you!"

¹⁸ When Naomi saw that she was determined to go with her, she said no more to her. ¹⁹ So the two of them went on until they came to Bethlehem. When they came to Bethlehem, the whole town was stirred because of them; and the women said, "Is this Naomi?" ²⁰ She said to them, "Call me no longer Naomi, call me Mara, for the Almighty has dealt bitterly with me. ²¹ I went away full, but the LORD has brought me back empty; why call me Naomi when the LORD has dealt harshly with me, and the Almighty has brought calamity upon me?" ²² So Naomi returned together with Ruth the Moabite, her daughter-in-law, who came back with her from the country of Moab. They came to Bethlehem at the beginning of the barley harvest.

2 Now Naomi had a kinsman on her husband's side, a prominent rich man, of the family of Elimelech, whose name was Boaz. ² And Ruth the Moabite said to Naomi, "Let me go to the field and glean among the ears of grain, behind someone in whose sight I may find favor." She said to her, "Go, my daughter." ³ So she went. She came and gleaned in the field behind the reapers. As it happened, she came to the part of the field belong-

ing to Boaz, who was of the family of Elimelech. ⁴ Just then Boaz came from Bethlehem. He said to the reapers, "The LORD be with you." They answered, "The LORD bless you." ⁵ Then Boaz said to his servant who was in charge of the reapers, "To whom does this young woman belong?" ⁶ The servant who was in charge of the reapers answered, "She is the Moabite who came back with Naomi from the country of Moab. ⁷ She said, 'Please, let me glean and gather among the sheaves behind the reapers.' So she came, and she has been on her feet from early this morning until now, without resting even for a moment." ⁸ Then Boaz said to Ruth, "Now listen, my daughter, do not go to glean in another field or leave this one, but keep close to my young women. ⁹ Keep your eyes on the field that is being reaped, and follow behind them. I have ordered the young men not to bother you. If you get thirsty, go to the vessels and drink from what the young men have drawn." ¹⁰ Then she fell prostrate, with her face to the ground, and said to him, "Why have I found favor in your sight, that you should take notice of me, when I am a foreigner?" ¹¹ But Boaz answered her, "All that you have done for your

mother-in-law since the death of your husband has been fully told me, and how you left your father and mother and your native land and came to a people that you did not know before. ¹² May the LORD reward you for your deeds, and may you have a full reward from the LORD, the God of Israel, under whose wings you have come for refuge!" ¹³ Then she said, "May I continue to find favor in your sight, my LORD, for you have comforted me and spoken kindly to your servant, even though I am not one of your servants."

¹⁴ At mealtime Boaz said to her, "Come here, and eat some of this bread, and dip your morsel in the sour wine." So she sat beside the reapers, and he heaped up for her some parched grain. She ate until she was satisfied, and she had some left over. ¹⁵ When she got up to glean, Boaz instructed his young men, "Let her glean even among the standing sheaves, and do not reproach her. ¹⁶ You must also pull out some handfuls for her from the bundles, and leave them for her to glean, and do not rebuke her."

¹⁷ So she gleaned in the field until evening. Then she beat out what she had gleaned, and it was about an ephah of barley. ¹⁸ She picked it up and came into the town, and her mother-in-law saw how much she had gleaned. Then she took out and gave her what was left over after she herself had been satisfied. ¹⁹ Her mother-in-law said to her, "Where did you glean today? And where have you worked? Blessed be the man who took notice of you." So she told her mother-in-law with whom she had worked, and said, "The name of the man with whom I worked today is Boaz." ²⁰ Then Naomi said to her daughter-in-law, "Blessed be he by the LORD, whose kindness has not forsaken the living or the dead!" Naomi also said to her, "The man is a relative of ours, one of our nearest kin." ²¹ Then Ruth the Moabite said, "He even said to me, 'Stay close by my servants, until they have finished all my harvest.'" ²² Naomi said to Ruth, her daughter-in-law, "It is better, my daughter, that you go out with his young women, otherwise you might be bothered in another field." ²³ So she stayed close to the young women of Boaz, gleaning until the end of the barley and wheat harvests; and she lived with her mother-in-law.

3 Naomi her mother-in-law said to her, "My daughter, I need to seek some security for you, so that it may be well with you. ² Now here is our kinsman Boaz, with whose young women you have been working. See, he is winnowing barley tonight at the threshing floor. ³ Now wash and anoint yourself, and put on your best clothes and go down to the threshing floor; but do not make yourself known to the man until he has finished eating and drinking. ⁴ When he lies down, observe the place where he lies; then, go and uncover his feet and lie down; and he will tell you what to do." ⁵ She said to her, "All that you tell me I will do."

⁶ So she went down to the threshing floor and did just as her mother-in-law had instructed her. ⁷ When Boaz had eaten and drunk, and he was in a contented mood, he went to lie down at the end of the heap of grain. Then she came stealthily and uncovered his feet, and lay down. ⁸ At midnight the man was startled, and turned over, and there, lying at his feet, was a woman! ⁹ He said, "Who are you?" And she answered, "I am Ruth, your servant; spread your cloak over your servant, for you are next-of-kin." ¹⁰ He said, "May you be blessed by the LORD, my daughter; this last instance of your loyalty is better than the first; you have not gone after young men, whether poor or rich. ¹¹ And now, my daughter, do not be afraid, I will do for you all that you ask, for all the assembly of my people know that you are a worthy woman. ¹² But now, though it is true that I am a near kinsman, there is another kinsman more closely related than I. ¹³ Remain this night, and in the morning, if he will act as next-of-kin for you, good; let him do it. If he is not willing to act as next-of-kin for you, then, as the LORD lives, I will act as next-of-kin for you. Lie down until the morning." ¹⁴ So she lay at his feet until morning, but got up before one person could recognize another; for he said, "It must not be known that the woman came to the threshing floor." ¹⁵ Then he said, "Bring the cloak you are wearing and hold it out." So she held it, and he measured out six measures of barley, and put it on her back; then he went into the city.

¹⁶ She came to her mother-in-law, who said, "How did things go with you, my daughter?" Then she told her all that the man had done for her, ¹⁷ saying, "He gave me these six measures of barley, for he said, 'Do not go back to your mother-in-law empty-handed.'" ¹⁸ She replied, "Wait, my daughter, until you learn how the matter turns out, for the man will not rest, but will settle the matter today."

Opposite: Naomi fears that her two widowed daughters-in-law will have difficulty finding new husbands in Judah, and therefore offers them friendly counsel: stay in your native land. Only Orpah agrees. Ruth is resolved to stay with Naomi wherever she might go. Painting by Salvador Dali (1904–1989).

4 No sooner had Boaz gone up to the gate and sat down there than the next-of-kin, of whom Boaz had spoken, came passing by. So Boaz said, "Come over, friend; sit down here." And he went over and sat down. 2 Then Boaz took ten men of the elders of the city, and said, "Sit down here"; so they sat down. 3 He then said to the next-of-kin, "Naomi, who has come back from the country of Moab, is selling the parcel of land that belonged to our kinsman Elimelech. 4 So I thought I would tell you of it, and say: Buy it in the presence of those sitting here, and in the presence of the elders of my people. If you will redeem it, redeem it; but if you will not, tell me, so that I may know; for there is no one prior to you to redeem it, and I come after you." So he said, "I will redeem it." 5 Then Boaz said, "The day you acquire the field from the hand of Naomi, you are also acquiring Ruth the Moabite, the widow of the dead man, to maintain the dead man's name on his inheritance." 6 At this, the next-of-kin said, "I cannot redeem it for myself without damaging my own inheritance. Take my right of redemption yourself, for I cannot redeem it."

13 So Boaz took Ruth and she became his wife. When they came together, the LORD made her conceive, and she bore a son. 14 Then the women said to Naomi, "Blessed be the LORD, who has not left you this day without next-of-kin; and may his name be renowned in Israel! 15 He shall be to you a restorer of life and a nourisher of your old age; for your daughter-in-law who loves you, who is more to you than seven sons, has borne him." 16 Then Naomi took the child and laid him in her bosom, and became his nurse. 17 The women of the neighborhood gave him a name, saying, "A son has been born to Naomi." They named him Obed; he became the father of Jesse, the father of David.

Nicolas Poussin (1594–1665) in this harvest painting entitled Summer *depicts Boaz, with his servants and maids, reaping the fields. Ruth has joined them, and Boaz advises his servants to deliberately leave extra gleanings for Ruth. Musée du Louvre, Paris*

The story of a friendship

Dorothee Soelle

Goethe praises the book of Ruth "because it pursues the lofty purpose of providing for a king of Israel decent, interesting ancestors, but can also be seen as the most charming little epic and idyllic story that has come down to us."

Starting with the "lofty purpose" of this little book: The Moabite Ruth, like Tamar and Rahab, belongs to those alien, non-Israelite ancestresses of David who join Israel and adopt its God on their own initiative and do their utmost to stay in the community of the chosen people. Famine and exile, settling in a foreign land, and the impediments to return constitute the social and historical background of this story. How do people survive such common disasters?

"Your people shall be my people, and your God my God" (Ruth 1:16) the Moabite Ruth says to her mother-in-law, the Israelite Naomi. Such an attitude is not the rule in a premodern, tribal-oriented, ethnocentric world, but the exception; this is why the narrator skillfully incorporates into the story another Moabite woman next to Ruth who turns the other way and stays with her people and its laws. Orpah ("who shows her nape, turning away") is persuaded by her mother-in-law to return. In this story, Naomi plays the part usually played by the patriarchs: the wise, kindly, experienced woman who cares for her daughters-in-law as if they were her own. She urges them to do the reasonable thing and to fulfill their expectations to find a home in the house of their husbands in their own land. Orpah, after tears and kisses, follows this advice. Ruth, who is deeply attached to the older woman, stays with her for the sake of mutual protection and caring.

The relationship between the two women, the Israelite Naomi who made Moab her home but returns after her husband's and her sons' deaths, and Ruth, whose name might best be interpreted as "woman friend," is one of the most beautiful stories of friendship in the Bible. It is no coincidence that Ruth's promise to her second mother is often taken out of context and applied to marriage relationship; as in the engagement motto: "for wither thou goest will go; and where thou lodgest, I will lodge" (Ruth 1:16 KJV). Here is a women's friendship based on reciprocity and respect, After Ruth has solemnly confirmed her resolve, the older woman simply keeps silence (Ruth 1:18). Unlike the struggle for power between Samson and Delilah—the latter incessantly working on her husband, talking, arguing, begging—this is a relationship of mutual dependence voluntarily chosen. The friendship between Naomi and Ruth is founded on both trust and respect. They are tied to one another by their weaknesses and their strength: Ruth the foreigner needs Naomi to gain a foothold in an alien country—which can only be realized in their world through matrimony or motherhood—and the aging Naomi, well aware of her isolation, can no longer go to the field to glean and needs active help from the younger woman. Both need each other's protection to survive in a man's world. Both are widows, a fact that diminishes their rights and deprives them of protection. The younger woman, Ruth, fears being molested by men at her place of work, while the older woman has to worry about simply maintaining herself. It is this solidarity between the women that lends to the story an unmistakable atmosphere of happiness and cheer, or, in the language of the eighteenth century, of the idyll.

What Tamar was forced to do by herself the two women do jointly, in a more civilized, less disreputable manner. The initiative is Naomi's; she envisages a marriage between Ruth and the rich, generous Boaz of Bethlehem. There is a legal basis for such a marriage as Boaz, a relative, is ideally suited to be the goel, or "kinsman redeemer" who brings back the forfeited inheritance by marrying the young heiress. It requires only a little push to call Boaz's attention to his legally prescribed role. This is where Naomi's trick comes in; there is a remote connection to Tamar's deception when she dressed and behaved like a whore to ensure her inclusion in the line of "mothers." Naomi, too, sends Ruth beautifully dressed (and at first in disguise) into the dark of the night to Boaz. But where Judah was deceived, Boaz acts as a responsible landed proprietor. After Ruth makes herself known to him, she asks him to spread his cloak, literally his "wings," over her. Covering another with one's coat was a Semitic custom by which one claimed property rights over a person and at the same time guaranteed protection for him or her. Thus the prophet says about God's ties

But Ruth said, "Do not press me to leave you or to turn back from following you!

Where you go, I will go; where you lodge, I will lodge; your people shall be my people, and your God my

God. Where you die, I will die—there will I be buried. May the Lord do thus and so to me, and more

as well, if even death parts me from you!"

Ruth 1:16–17

Naomi and Her Two Daughers-in-Law *by the
English poet and artist William Blake (1757–1827).
Naomi had suggested to her widowed daughters-in-
law Ruth and Orpah that she return to Judah by
herself. As this painting shows, Ruth resolved to
stay with Naomi and never to leave her.
Victoria and Albert Museum, London*

to Jerusalem: "I passed by you again and looked on you; you were at the age for love. I spread the edge of my cloak over you, and covered your nakedness: I pledged myself to you and entered into a covenant with you ... and you became mine" (Ezek. 16:8). Ruth, in asking Boaz to "spread your cloak over your servant" asks him to marry her;

and shortly thereafter the marriage is concluded at "the gate" where civil matters are decided.

The story could end here, but then it would not be so much the story of women and their relation to one another. When Ruth has given birth to Boaz's child, Naomi appears once more, and the term "nearest kin" first applied to Ruth

(Ruth 2:20) is now given to Naomi, and the curse of dying childless is taken from her. And once more, the story turns back to the main theme of friendship between two women: "Your daughter-in-law, who loves you, who is more to you than seven sons, has borne him [the future grandfather of King David]" (Ruth 4:15). Naomi takes the child and lays it on her bosom—which could be interpreted as a kind of adoption—and becomes his nurse. The neighbors, now emerging like a Greek chorus at the end of the story, declare: "A son has been born to Naomi" (Ruth 4:17). And the women are the ones who give the child his name.

Four illustrations from the Bible Moralisée *of the Codex Vindobonensis 2554, fol. 34v (early thirteenth century) presenting the story of Ruth and Boaz. From top to bottom: Boaz covers the sleeping Ruth with his coat; Boaz takes off one of the next-of-kin's shoes as a legal symbol that Boaz has now become Ruth's protector; Boaz marries Ruth; Ruth and Boaz have a son who will become the grandfather of King David.*
Oesterreichische Nationalbibliothek, Vienna

Opposite: Painting by Marc Chagall (1887–1985). Naomi advises her Moabite daughters-in-law to stay in their home country and let her move back to Judah alone.
Musée national du message biblique, Nizza

Marc Chagall

Ancient and medieval sources

Joe H. Kirchberger

The time of this story's composition is not known. It was once assumed that it was written in the period following the exile, as a kind of protest against the orthodox politics of the post-exilic leaders Ezra and Nehemiah who forbade mixed marriages, for instance with Moabites. The message of the book is clearly that one's lineage is less important than character and religious devotion. But more recently scholars have come to believe that the book was written much earlier, during the time of the kings. This is indicated by the fact that no king is mentioned after David. Neither can the story be pure invention: one would hardly have deliberately attributed a pagan ancestress to the royal house and to the future Messiah.

IN JEWISH LEGEND Naomi (or Noëmi or Noomi) is called an Ammonite. This would make both Naomi and her daughters-in-law Orpah and Ruth descendants of Lot's daughters. At any rate, the giant Goliath, famous for his later fight with David, was said to be a son of Orpah. When Orpah separated from Ruth, she is said to have walked with her the last forty steps and in parting shed four tears. This is why, say the legends, her son Goliath was permitted to display his strength for forty days, and Orpah was blessed with four giant sons.

As soon as she had separated from Ruth, Orpah reverted to her old superstitions, for she, in contrast to Ruth, had adopted the Jewish faith for practical reasons only, not out of conviction. She also lived in sin. In the end, she was killed by one Abishai whom she herself had threatened to kill. Abishai was said to be on his way to David, who had been forced into a winepress by Ishbi, the giant brother of Goliath, to avenge his brother's death. God had deprived David of his strength to punish him for his sin with Bathsheba.

The husbands of Orpah and Ruth, Mahlon and Chilion, died young as a result of the sins of their father Elimelech, a very miserly man. According to some Jewish legends, David is supposed to have said to dying Goliath: "Your mother was Orpah who accepted the faith of the Philistines, but my mother (or rather, ancestress) was Ruth who adopted the true faith." Goliath's forty days of splendor have been connected by some interpreters with the forty days during which the people of Israel received God's laws in the desert.

Jewish legend suggests that God had included Ruth in his designs for a long time. For at the time of Moses he had ordered Israel to wage war against the Midianites and the Moabites, and Moses did move against them, but only David fought the Moabites. There were three reasons for this: first, Moab felt hostile toward Israel since Israel was always threatening to ransack the Moabites; second, whereas the Moabites wanted to kill the Israelites, the Midianites wanted to seduce them to sin, and that was a worse threat; third: God said, "Delay the war against Moab, for I have lost something valuable there. As soon as I have found it again, you may take your revenge on Moab." The veiled reference was to Ruth.

The famine in Israel that had driven Elimelech and his family to Moab had been sent by God to his people as punishment for their sins. Not only was bread scarce, but so also was God's word. Miserly Elimelech had done nothing to help his fellow tribesmen. Since he was very wealthy, his sons were made officers of high ranking in the Moabite army. They are even said to have married the daughters of the king of Moab. But then they were reduced to poverty and died young.

When Naomi decided to return, she foresaw that her Moabite daughters-in-law would be looked down upon in Israel, particularly because in Jerusalem each class of the population had to live in its own district. Yet she could not return home fast enough. Though barefoot and in rags, she walked incessantly, even on Sabbath days.

Ruth's first request to be allowed to accompany Naomi had to be rejected. According to law, a new convert could be accepted only if she asked twice. Naomi also warned Ruth of all the inconveniences in store for her: she would have to observe the Sabbath and all holidays and would not be allowed to go to the theater or the circus as she was accustomed to. But nothing could deter Ruth.

Opposite: Ruth with her son Obed, one of the frescoes of Michelangelo (1475–1564) in the Sistine Chapel showing Christ's ancestors. Ruth, the Moabite, is the ancestress of Jesus through her son who became the grandfather of King David.

Some sources say that Naomi and Ruth arrived in Bethlehem on the very day the wife of Boaz was buried. According to other versions, however, it was the first day of Passover. Boaz was amazed when Ruth never picked up grain although his people had dropped more than two sheaves; for that is what the law of the poor prescribes. She had come to his field because an angel had led her there. When he commended her for having converted to the Jewish faith, she replied: "Your ancestors did not take any pleasure in Timnah (the wife of Eliphaz, son of Esau) although she was of royal blood. And I belong only to a lowly people despised by God and excluded from Israel's community." But at that moment a voice from heaven reminded Boaz that only male members of the Moabite and Ammonite tribes were excluded from Israel, a fact that he in turn communicated to Ruth.

She is said to have called herself Boaz's servant, but he told her: "You will be seen as one of Israel's mothers, and kings and prophets will come from your womb." He also arranged for a dignified funeral for Elimelech and his sons.

When Boaz, coming from Bethlehem, greeted his reapers, "The LORD may be with you!" and when they answered him accordingly, heaven must have sanctioned these words, for normally God's name was never to be mentioned on weekdays. God blessed the few sheaves of grain Ruth had been given by Boaz so that she had enough to eat. Boaz even ordered his men to drop additional sheaves for Ruth to pick up. But she took only the bare essentials. When this happened day after day, Naomi became suspicious, assuming that Ruth had a lover in the field who helped her to the grain. When she became convinced that her suspicion was unfounded, she believed that Boaz and Ruth were planning a secret marriage. She tried to get the secret out of Ruth, but Ruth knew nothing about it. Naomi conceived a plan to send Ruth to Boaz at night. Ruth did go along, but was afraid to walk the road in the dark and decorated herself much

less than Naomi had suggested. She did not want to catch the attention of the young men she would meet on the road.

Boaz was a man of simple habits. Though he was affluent and eighty years old, he slept on the barn floor. When he discovered Ruth next to him, he first believed her to be a demon. She put him at ease: "You are the descendant of princes and an honorable man, but I, in the prime of my life, had to leave my home country where idolatry is being practiced, and here I am constantly pursued by lascivious young men. That is why I came to you, my savior, so that you may spread your cloak over me." According to most legends, Boaz resisted all temptations and said to her, "If my older brother Tob (who is not mentioned by name in the Bible) does not want you, I shall make myself your protector."

The following day Boaz went to the Sanhedrin, the highest legal and religious administrative office of the Jews, to settle this matter. Tob appeared very soon, for an angel had led him there. As he was not familiar with the Torah, he did not know that the prohibition of marrying Moabites referred only to men, and therefore refused to marry Ruth. So Boaz took her as his wife. By then, Ruth was forty years of age, and that they had a son at their respective ages can be explained only as a miracle. Naomi, who in her youth had been Ruth's nurse, was now made nurse to Obed, her grandson.

JOSEPHUS'S VERSION IS typically closer to the Bible itself. According to him, Orpah did not want to separate from Naomi either until Naomi implored her not to leave her home country. Following Ruth 4:1–10, he observes that before the council of the elders, the unnamed "next-of-kin" is at first quite ready to take over Elimelech's inheritance, until Boaz calls to his attention the fact that in this case he would have to marry Mahlon's widow. Thereupon he changed his decision. Naomi called Ruth's son Obed (meaning "servant"), says Josephus, because she raised him to take care of her in her old age.

Opposite: Painting by Marc Chagall (1887–1985). After her day's work in the field, Ruth brings to Naomi a surprisingly large share of grain and of barley Boaz had given her also. Musée national du message biblique, Nizza

Marc Chagall

Abigail

TRIUMPH OF PRUDENCE

1 Samuel
Chapter 25, verses 1–44

Above: Abigail, "clever and beautiful," from Bible Moralisée of the Codex Vindobonensis 2554, fol. 41, early thirteenth century. Oesterreichische Nationalbibliothek, Vienna

Opposite: The meeting of David and Abigail by Albrecht Altdorfer (ca. 1480–1538). Abigail has come to assuage David's wrath against her husband, a brutal, ambitious man who has disregarded all rules of hospitality, by speaking diplomatically and offering ample presents.
Kupferstichkabinett, Preußischer Kulturbesitz, Berlin

Now Samuel died; and all Israel assembled and mourned for him. They buried him at his home in Ramah.

Then David got up and went down to the wilderness of Paran. 2 There was a man in Maon, whose property was in Carmel. The man was very rich; he had three thousand sheep and a thousand goats. He was shearing his sheep in Carmel. 3 Now the name of the man was Nabal, and the name of his wife Abigail. The woman was clever and beautiful but the man was surly and mean; he was a Calebite. 4 David heard in the wilderness that Nabal was shearing his sheep. 5 So David sent ten young men; and David said to the young men, "Go up to Carmel, and go to Nabal, and greet him in my name. 6 Thus you shall salute him: 'Peace be to you, and peace be to your house, and peace be to all that you have. 7 I hear that you have shearers; now your shepherds have been with us, and we did them no harm, and they missed nothing, all the time they were in Carmel. 8 Ask your young men, and they will tell you. Therefore let my young men find favor in your sight; for we have come on a feast day. Please give whatever you have at hand to your servants and to your son David.'"

9 When David's young men came, they said all this to Nabal in the name of David; and then they waited. 10 But Nabal answered David's servants, "Who is David? Who is the son of Jesse? There are many servants today who are breaking away from their masters. 11 Shall I take my bread and my water and the meat that I have butchered for my shearers, and give it to men who come from I do not know where?" 12 So David's young men turned away, and came back and told him all this. 13 David said to his men, "Every man strap on his sword!" And every one of them strapped on his sword; David also strapped on his sword; and about four hundred men went up after David, while two hundred remained with the baggage. 14 But one of the young men told Abigail, Nabal's wife, "David sent messengers out of the wilderness to salute our master, and he shouted insults at them. 15 Yet the men were very good to us, and we suffered no harm, and we never missed anything when we were in the fields, as long as we were with them; 16 they were a wall to us both by night and by day, all the while we were with them keeping the sheep. 17 Now therefore know this and consider what you should do; for evil has been decided against our master and against all his house; he is so ill-natured that no one can speak to him." 18 Then Abigail hurried and took two hundred loaves, two skins of wine, five sheep ready dressed, five measures of parched grain,

one hundred clusters of raisins, and two hundred cakes of figs. She loaded them on donkeys [19] and said to her young men, "Go on ahead of me; I am coming after you." But she did not tell her husband Nabal. [20] As she rode on the donkey and came down under cover of the mountain, David and his men came down toward her; and she met them. [21] Now David had said, "Surely it was in vain that I protected all that this fellow has in the wilderness, so that nothing was missed of all that belonged to him; but he has returned me evil for good. [22] God do so to David and more also, if by morning I leave so much as one male of all who belong to him." [23] When Abigail saw David, she hurried and alighted from the donkey, fell before David on her face, bowing to the ground. [24] She fell at his feet and said, "Upon me alone, my lord, be the guilt; please let your servant speak in your ears, and hear the words of your servant. [25] My lord, do not take seriously this ill-natured fellow, Nabal; for as his name is, so is he; Nabal is his name, and folly is with him; but I, your servant, did not see the young men of my lord, whom you sent. [26] Now then, my lord, as the LORD lives, and as you yourself live, since the LORD has restrained you from bloodguilt and from taking vengeance with your own hand, now let your enemies and those who seek to do evil to my lord be like Nabal. [27] And now let this present that your servant has brought to my lord be given to the young men who follow my lord. [28] Please forgive the trespass of your servant; for the LORD will certainly make my lord a sure house, because my lord is fighting the battles of the LORD; and evil shall not be found in you so long as you live. [29] If anyone should rise up to pursue you and to seek your life, the life of my lord shall be bound in the bundle of the living under the care of the LORD your God; but the lives of your enemies he shall sling out as from the hollow of a sling. [30] When the LORD has done to my lord according to all the good that he has spoken concerning you, and has appointed you prince over Israel, [31] my lord shall have no cause of grief, or pangs of conscience, for having shed blood without cause or for having saved himself. And when the LORD has dealt well with my lord, then remember your servant." [32] David said to Abigail, "Blessed be the LORD, the God of Israel, who sent you to meet me today! [33] Blessed be your good sense, and blessed be you, who have kept me today from bloodguilt and from avenging myself by my own hand! [34] For as surely as the LORD the God of Israel lives, who has restrained me from hurting you, unless you had hurried and come to meet me, truly by morning there would not have been left to Nabal so much as one male." [35] Then David received from her hand what she had brought him; he said to her, "Go up to your house in peace; see, I have heeded your voice, and I have granted your petition." [36] Abigail came to Nabal; he was holding a feast in his house, like the feast of a king. Nabal's heart was merry within him, for he was very drunk; so she told him nothing at all until the morning light. [37] In the morning, when the wine had gone out of Nabal, his wife told him these things, and his heart died within him; he became like a stone. [38] About ten days later the LORD struck Nabal, and he died.

[39] When David heard that Nabal was dead, he said, "Blessed be the LORD who has judged the case of Nabal's insult to me, and has kept back his servant from evil; the LORD has returned the evil-doing of Nabal upon his own head." Then David sent and wooed Abigail, to make her his wife. [40] When David's servants came to Abigail at Carmel, they said to her, "David has sent us to you to take you to him as his wife." [41] She rose and bowed down, with her face to the ground, and said, "Your servant is a slave to wash the feet of the servants of my lord." [42] Abigail got up hurriedly and rode away on a donkey; her five maids attended her. She went after the messengers of David and became his wife. [43] David also married Ahinoam of Jezreel; both of them became his wives. [44] Saul had given his daughter Michal, David's wife, to Palti son of Laish, who was from Gallim.

*Above: Abigail kneels before David on horseback.
She asks him to accept food she has brought and
to forgive her husband who in his drunkenness
violated the laws of hospitality. Miniature from
the* Miroir de l'Humaine Salvation, *MS 139/1363,
fol. 38 v, dating to the fifteenth century.
Musée Condé, Chantilly*

*Pages 74–75: The Dutch painter David Teniers
the Elder (1582–1649) puts the meeting between
Abigail and David in a wide landscape with beautiful trees. Abigail kneels amid the gifts of food
spread around her as tokens of reconciliation.
David and his soldiers, clad in magnificent baroque
attire, do not much resemble the poor, harassed
men described in the Bible.
Rafael Valls Gallery, London*

Life in the desert

Dorothee Soelle

The story of Abigail, which is in the center of the twenty-fifth chapter of the first book of Samuel, is a farcical depiction of customs in the desert, told with a touch of biting irony. It takes place before David became king. One sees here the astute marriages by which the future sovereign establishes advantageous relationships with the richest and most honored families in Judah. The story is presented as a patriarchal one with reversed roles. Nabal is a cattle owner at the foot of Mount Carmel, wealthy but stupid, his wife beautiful and intelligent. He is miserly and brutal, she, clever and generous. He drinks himself unconscious, she saves land and life for herself and her people at that time. The name Nabal means "fool" or "moron"; and his tribe, the Calebites, was considered especially uncouth and vulgar.

In the tradition of nomadic peoples there is always a great festival at the time of sheepshearing. David, roaming about the desert with his men, uses this opportunity to demand tribute from the rich cattle owners to which he is entitled by the law of the desert. A bedouin sheik takes over the "protections" of the neighboring farmers or half-nomads and therefore considers a share of their harvest as a "wage" to which he has a legal claim; similar situations may still exist today. This legal give-and-take—protection from aggression and theft against more or less voluntary contributions—also explains why David's messengers address Nabal as "brother." "Brother" is the nonalien with whom family-type relations have already been established. So visiting Nabal at the sheep-shearing festival serves the purpose of the roaming nomads to put in their demand for tribute from the settler. The festival connected with the shearing also provides an occasion for hospitality, and to deny participation in the feast is a gross violation of hospitality. In a well-worded speech in the ancient Near Eastern manner, David's men—no less than ten, which implies something of a menace—demand what is coming to them from Nabal, the vulgar boor! He, in turn, ridicules the messengers and their leader, calls them beggars and rabble, and ignores the rules of protection and trust, and of hospitality. He has, as David puts it in accordance with legal tradition, "returned me evil for good" (1 Sam. 25:21). Indignantly, David breaks camp, resolved to take revenge. "So and more also do God unto the enemies of David, if I leave of all that pertain to him by the morning light any that pisseth against the wall" (1 Sam. 25:22 KJV). This coarse, masculine tirade is in sharp contrast to what follows in the reconciliation achieved by the clever diplomacy of a woman.

Abigail acts quickly and effectively. She grasps the deadly menace at once, and knows as well as her servants that there is no use talking to her husband. Without saying a word to him, she has her asses loaded up richly—one could ask how she came by two hundred cakes of figs in such a hurry—and moves to meet David on her own authority. The narrator has arranged the story quite skillfully, in citing David's vow to kill all of Nabal's men just at the moment when the two dissimilar caravans meet. David and his men are on a revenge and looting expedition of warriors; Abigail with her heavily loaded asses undertakes a peace mission. Before a word is spoken, the gestures of beautiful Abigail do some talking. Quickly she dismounts from her donkey, throws herself on her face at David's feet, and follows up with an artful speech. She calls the warrior "my lord," and refers to herself who lies in the dust before him as "your servant." She assumes all responsibility for the shameful treatment of the messengers; she is to blame, for her husband is a fool and will always be one. Her speech practically disables David legally. She cleverly points at the presents she has brought along for David's soldiers, but her religious argument is even more eloquent: so far God has saved David from staining his hands with blood, and he will continue to establish and strengthen his rule without David having to resort to evil, or vengeful acts.

David replies in the same manner, skillfully combining theological arguments with his personal interest. Certainly God has sent Abigail to prevent him from spilling blood and taking into his own hands the revenge that God has reserved for himself. He bids her to leave in peace and to return home.

The story might end here, having served as an introduction to David's future kingship. But Abigail's independent action has yet to be brought to Nabal's attention. He—and this is where the

burlesque elements of the story come into play—lies dead drunk after the great festival, realizing neither the danger he had brought upon himself nor his salvation through Abigail's wit and initiative. When Abigail recounts the story to him, he becomes "like a stone," and ten days later the Lord smites him and he dies. As David says when he hears the news, the Lord has turned Nabal's wickedness back upon his own head.

Now David can marry beautiful Abigail. Already in their first meeting there had been erotic undertones: self-accusation, imploring, humility and empathy, adoration and the prospect of happiness were part of the coded message from a beautiful and clever woman to a hero and future king. Now all that remains is a declaration of love. David sends his suitors to Abigail; the wealthy widow will hear nothing of presents or negotiations. She bows down deeply, and then "gets up hurriedly" (1 Sam. 25:42); she has not only saved her possessions and her integrity but also gotten rid of the rich, moronic Nabal for the shining hero. Nabal the fool is overcome. Not only that, however: generosity overcomes stinginess, conces-

sion overcomes stubbornness, respect for customs overcomes self-seeking. Abigail's flexibility and diplomacy also prevent a mindless attack from the other man, David. The woman between two men pursues a better policy without weapons and makes peace.

The Spanish painter Juan Antonio Escalante (ca. 1630–1670), an admirer of Tintoretto, whose style is recognizable in this painting, shows David graciously accepting Abigail's presents of reconciliation. In the meeting of their eyes, a spark of erotic interest can be sensed between the two, which will later prompt David's courting Abigail after Nabal's death.
Museo del Prado, Madrid

Above: Abigail lies humbly on the ground before David, who is surrounded by his soldiers. The servants behind her are carrying presents designed to make David forget her husband's vile miserliness. Ilja Jefimowich Repin (1844–1930), the most prominent historical painter of modern Russia, has painted this scene in realistic detail. Biblioteca Apostolica Vaticana, Vatican

Right: First meeting of David and Abigail. She rode to David without her husband's knowledge to give him presents and to reconcile David to her husband, who had arrogantly refused him any hospitality. Illustration from the Biblia Pauperum, *Codex Germanicus 155, fol. 23v. Bayerische Staatsbibliothek, Munich*

Ancient and medieval sources

Joe H. Kirchberger

Abigail—the meaning of the name is "the father's joy"—is supposed to have been one of the four most beautiful women in history, the others being Sarah, Rahab, and Esther. The mere thought of her is said to have excited men. Not only was she clever and a gifted prophetess, but she was also a good diplomat. She offered her presents to David very tactfully and also is said to have told him that a death verdict against a man (in this case Nabal) could be pronounced only in daytime, not at night. When David answered that a rebel like Nabal was not entitled to protection by the law, she told him, "Saul is still alive, so you are not yet the recognized lord of the world." Her remark about avoiding "blood guiltiness" in 1 Samuel 25:31 is supposed to allude to David's future adventure with Bathsheba, thus authenticating her prophetic gifts. Talmudic interpreters have objected to her imploring David to "remember your servant"; as a married woman she was not permitted to say such a thing. But she had the courage to take all blame upon herself, and as a result David did not carry out his vow against Nabal (as Rebekah had once taken all responsibility when Esau was deceived). After she had become David's wife, she bore him a son who was called Chileab, meaning "like the father" (in 1 Chron. 3:1 he is called Daniel). The legends record that he grew up to be a very learned man and was among the select few who were taken into Paradise when still alive. Abigail herself heads the fifth of seven groups of women in Paradise, next to Sarah, Rachel, and Rebekah. Nabal, whose name means "fool," was not just arrogant and coarse, but also very miserly. His lands were in Carmel, but he lived in Maon. When the poor came to him in Maon, he sent them to Carmel, and vice versa. He wanted only to be rid of them. He was also very proud of his ancestors, for he traced his origin back to Judah and to Caleb, Joshua's companion, and looked down on David as a descendant of the Moabite Ruth, denying him any right to the throne. His question, "Who is the son of Jesse?" and his reference to the many servants who had left David was all the more insulting, as his latter statement had some basis in truth.

In Josephus's rendition the biblical narrative is further embellished. He claims that David had given specific orders to his men not to touch Nabal's flocks even in an emergency, for that would be a crime against God. Nabal's reaction was therefore all the more unexpected. Josephus puts it this way: "This is how they think of themselves, these men who have run away from their proper master and now behave in an unseemly and arrogant fashion." When Abigail set out to meet David, Nabal is said to have been dead drunk. Then Abigail said to David, "He will not go unpunished even if you abstain from killing him; and he will be punished by those who are ill disposed towards you. And the misfortune awaiting him will revert to your enemies' heads." When David learned of Nabal's death, he concluded that he had perished by his own meanness, and that all evil people are thus chastised by God; God is concerned with every individual and treats people, both good and bad, according to their merits.

Now the name of the man was Nabal,

and the name of his wife Abigail.

The woman was clever and beautiful, but the man was surly and mean;

he was a Calebite.

1 Samuel 25:3

Judith

SAVIOR OF HER PEOPLE

Judith

Chapter 8, verses 1–36; Chapter 9, verses 1–14
Chapter 10, verses 1–23; Chapter 11, verses 1–23
Chapter 12, verses 1–20; Chapter 13, verses 1–20

The story of Judith is set in the time of King Nebuchadnezzar (ca. 605–562 B.C.) but was written down only at the time of the Maccabean wars in the second century B.C. The author of the story was more interested in describing Judith's heroic deeds than in historical correctness: Nebuchadnezzar ruled in Babylon, not in Assyria, and the city of Nineveh where he is made to reign had already been destroyed by his father, Nabopolassar. Judith's hometown of Bethulia has never been identified.

Then Judith said to them,

"Listen to me. I am about to do something that

will go down through all generations of our

descendants."

Judith 8:32

8 Now in those days Judith heard about these things: she was the daughter of Merari son of Ox son of Joseph son of Oziel son of Elkiah son of Ananias son of Gideon son of Raphain son of Ahitub son of Elijah son of Hilkiah son of Eliab son of Nathanael son of Salamiel son of Sarasadai son of Israel. ² Her husband Manasseh, who belonged to her tribe andfamily, had died during the barley harvest. ³ For as he stood overseeing those who were binding sheaves in the field, he was overcome by the burning heat, and took to his bed and died in his town Bethulia. So they buried him with his ancestors in the field between Dothan and Balamon. ⁴ Judith remained as a widow for three years and four months ⁵ at home where she set up a tent for herself on the roof of her house. She put sackcloth around her waist and dressed in widow's clothing. ⁶ She fasted all the days of her widowhood, except the day before the sabbath and the sabbath itself, the day before the new moon and the day of the new moon, and the festivals and days of rejoicing of the house of Israel. ⁷ She was beautiful in appearance, and was very lovely to behold. Her husband Manasseh had left her gold and silver, men and women slaves, livestock, and fields; and she maintained this estate. ⁸ No one spoke ill of her, for she feared God with great devotion.

⁹ When Judith heard the harsh words spoken by the people against the ruler, because they were faint for lack of water, and when she heard all that Uzziah said to them, and how he promised them under oath to surrender the town to the Assyrians after five days, ¹⁰ she sent her maid, who was in charge of all she possessed, to summon Uzziah and Chabris and Charmis, the elders of her town. ¹¹ They came to her, and she said to them, "Listen to me, rulers of the people of Bethulia! What you have said to the people today is not right; you have even sworn and pronounced this oath between God and you, promising to surrender the town to our enemies unless the Lord turns and helps us within so many days. ¹² Who are you to put God to the test today, and to set yourselves up in the place of God in human affairs? ¹³ You are putting the Lord Almighty to the test, but you will never learn anything! ¹⁴ You cannot plumb the depths of the human heart or understand the workings of the human mind; how do you expect to search out God, who made all these things, and find out his mind or comprehend his thought? No, my brothers, do not anger the Lord our God. ¹⁵ For if he does not choose to help us within these five days, he has power to protect us within any time he pleases, or even to destroy us in the presence of our enemies. ¹⁶ Do not try to bind the purposes of the Lord our

דר שטיריכר

Above: After the sumptuous feast, the servants fall asleep, leaving Judith alone with Holofernes who, himself overcome by wine, falls into bed. She recognizes the opportunity to execute her plans. Codex hebr. 37, fol. 81a r, 1428. Staats- und Universitätsbibliothek, Hamburg

Right: Holofernes is amazed by the Hebrew woman's eloquence as she approaches him without inhibition. He says to her, "Take courage, woman. No one will hurt you." Add. MS 11639, fol. 121a r. British Library, London

God; for God is not like a human being, to be threatened, or like a mere mortal, to be won over by pleading. 17 Therefore, while we wait for his deliverance, let us call upon him to help us, and he will hear our voice, if it pleases him. 18 "For never in our generation, nor in these present days, has there been any tribe or family or people or town of ours that worships gods made with hands, as was done in days gone by. 19 That was why our ancestors were handed over to the sword and to pillage, and so they suffered a great catastrophe before our enemies. 20 But we know no other god but him, and so we hope that he will not disdain us or any of our nation.

21 For if we are captured, all Judea will be captured and our sanctuary will be plundered; and he will make us pay for its desecration with our blood. 22 The slaughter of our kindred and the captivity of the land and the desolation of our inheritance—all this he will bring on our heads among the Gentiles, wherever we serve as slaves; and we shall be an offense and a disgrace in the eyes of those who acquire us. 23 For our slavery will not bring us into favor, but the Lord our God will turn it to dishonor. 24 "Therefore, my brothers, let us set an example for our kindred, for their lives depend upon us, and the sanctuary—both the temple and the altar—rests upon us.

25 In spite of everything let us give thanks to the Lord our God, who is putting us to the test as he did our ancestors. 26 Remember what he did with Abraham, and how he tested Isaac, and what happened to Jacob in Syrian Mesopotamia, while he was tending the sheep of Laban, his mother's brother. 27 For he has not tried us with fire, as he did them, to search their hearts, nor has he taken vengeance on us; but the Lord scourges those who are close to him in order to admonish them."

28 Then Uzziah said to her, "All that you have said was spoken out of a true heart, and there is no one who can deny your words. 29 Today is not the first time your wisdom has been shown, but from the beginning of your life all the people have recognized your understanding, for your heart's disposition is right. 30 But the people were so thirsty that they compelled us to do for them what we have promised, and made us take an oath that we cannot break. 31 Now since you are a God-fearing woman, pray for us, so that the Lord may send us rain to fill our cisterns. Then we will no longer feel faint from thirst." 32 Then Judith said to them, "Listen to me. I am about to do something that will go down through all generations of our descendants. 33 Stand at the town gate tonight so that I may go out with my maid; and within the days after which you have promised to surrender the town to our enemies, the Lord will deliver Israel by my hand. 34 Only, do not try to find out what I am doing; for I will not tell you until I have finished what I am about to do." 35 Uzziah and the rulers said to her, "Go in peace, and may the Lord God go before you, to take vengeance on our enemies." 36 So they returned from the tent and went to their posts.

9 Then Judith prostrated herself, put ashes on her head, and uncovered the sackcloth she was wearing. At the very time when the evening incense was being offered in the house of God in Jerusalem, Judith cried out to the Lord with a loud voice, and said,

Judith's prayer, which follows in verses 2–14, is shown on page 85.

10 When Judith had stopped crying out to the God of Israel, and had ended all these words, 2 she rose from where she lay prostrate. She called her maid and went down into the house where she lived on sabbaths and on her festal days. 3 She removed the sackcloth she had been wearing, took off her widow's garments, bathed her body with water, and anointed herself with precious ointment. She combed her hair, put on a tiara, and dressed herself in the festive attire that she used to wear while her husband Manasseh was living. 4 She put sandals on her feet, and put on her anklets, bracelets, rings, earrings, and all her other jewelry. Thus she made herself very beautiful, to entice the eyes of all the men who might see her. 5 She gave her maid a skin of wine and a flask of oil, and filled a bag with roasted grain, dried fig cakes, and fine bread; then she wrapped up all her dishes and gave them to her to carry.

6 Then they went out to the town gate of Bethulia and found Uzziah standing there with the elders of the town, Chabris and Charmis. 7 When they saw her transformed in appearance and dressed differently, they were very greatly astounded at her beauty and said to her, 8 "May the God of our ancestors grant you favor and fulfill your plans, so that the people of Israel may glory and Jerusalem may be exalted." She bowed down to God.

Opposite: On the fourth day, the gorgeously attired general of King Nebuchadnezzar invites Judith to his dinner table. She alone is seated at the table while the courtiers are standing. She, the Jewess, is allowed to serve him the dishes, showing that she possesses his complete confidence. Detail of a painting by Lucas Cranach the Elder (1472–1553). Schlossmuseum, Gotha

She put sandals on her feet, and put on her anklets, bracelets, rings, earrings, and all her other jewelry. Thus she made herself very beautiful, to entice the eyes of all the men who might see her.

Judith 10:4

PRAYER OF JUDITH
Judith 9:2–14

"O Lord God of my ancestor Simeon, to whom you gave a sword to take revenge on those strangers who had torn off a virgin's clothing to defile her, and exposed her thighs to put her to shame, and polluted her womb to disgrace her; for you said, 'It shall not be done'—yet they did it. [3] So you gave up their rulers to be killed, and their bed, which was ashamed of the deceit they had practiced, was stained with blood, and you struck down slaves along with princes, and princes on their thrones. [4] You gave up their wives for booty and their daughters to captivity, and all their booty to be divided among your beloved children who burned with zeal for you and abhorred the pollution of their blood and called on you for help—O God, my God, hear me also—a widow.

[5] "For you have done these things and those that went before and those that followed. You have designed the things that are now, and those that are to come. What you had in mind has happened; [6] the things you decided on presented themselves and said, 'Here we are!' For all your ways are prepared in advance, and your judgment is with foreknowledge.

[7] "Here now are the Assyrians, a greatly increased force, priding themselves in their horses and riders, boasting in the strength of their foot soldiers, and trusting in shield and spear, in bow and sling. They do not know that you are the lord who crushes wars; the lord is your name. [8] Break their strength by your might, and bring down their power in your anger; for they intend to defile your sanctuary, and to pollute the tabernacle where your glorious name resides, and to break off the horns of your altar with the sword. [9] Look at their pride, and send your wrath upon their heads. Give to me, a widow, the strong hand to do what I plan. [10] By the deceit of my lips strike down the slave with the prince and the prince with his servant; crush their arrogance by the hand of a woman.

[11] "For your strength does not depend on numbers, nor your might on the powerful. But you are the God of the lowly, helper of the oppressed, upholder of the weak, protector of the forsaken, savior of those without hope. [12] Please, please, God of my father, God of the heritage of Israel, lord of heaven and earth, Creator of the waters, King of all your creation, hear
my prayer! [13] Make my deceitful words bring wound and bruise on those who have planned cruel things against your covenant, and against your sacred house, and against Mount Zion, and against the house your children possess. [14] Let your whole nation and every tribe know and that you are God, the God of all power and might, and that there is no other who protects the people of Israel but you alone!"

9 Then she said to them, "Order the gate of the town to be opened for me so that I may go out and accomplish the things you have just said to me." So they ordered the young men to open the gate for her, as she requested. 10 When they had done this, Judith went out, accompanied by her maid. The men of the town watched her until she had gone down the mountain and passed through the valley, where they lost sight of her.

11 As the women were going straight on through the valley, an Assyrian patrol met her 12 and took her into custody. They asked her, "To what people do you belong, and where are you coming from, and where are you going?" She replied, "I am a daughter of the Hebrews, but I am fleeing from them, for they are about to be handed over to you to be devoured. 13 I am on my way to see Holofernes the commander of your army, to give him a true report; I will show him a way by which he can go and capture all the hill country without losing one of his men, captured or slain." 14 When the men heard her words, and observed her face— she was in their eyes marvelously beautiful—they said to her, 15 "You have saved your life by hurrying down to see our Lord. Go at once to his tent; some of us will escort you and hand you over to him. 16 When you stand before him, have no fear in your heart, but tell him what you have just said, and he will treat you well." 17 They chose from their number a hundred men to accompany her and her maid, and they brought them to the tent of Holofernes. 18 There was great excitement in the whole camp, for her arrival was reported from tent to tent. They came and gathered around her as she stood outside the tent of Holofernes, waiting until they told him about her. 19 They marveled at her beauty and admired the Israelites, judging them by her. They said to one another, "Who can despise these people, who have women like this among them? It is not wise to leave one of their men alive, for if we let them go they will be able to beguile the whole world!"

20 Then the guards of Holofernes and all his servants came out and led her into the tent. 21 Holofernes was resting on his bed under a canopy that was woven with purple and gold, emeralds and other precious stones. 22 When they told him of her, he came to the front of the tent,

Opposite: Jan Massys (1509–1575) shows Judith, having used her feminine charms to make Holofernes overconfident so that she could decapitate him in his sleep.
Musée du Louvre, Paris

with silver lamps carried before him. 23 When Judith came into the presence of Holofernes and his servants, they all marveled at the beauty of her face. She prostrated herself and did obeisance to him, but his slaves raised her up.

11 Then Holofernes said to her, "Take courage, woman, and do not be afraid in your heart, for I have never hurt anyone who chose to serve Nebuchadnezzar, king of all the earth. 2 Even now, if your people who live in the hill country had not slighted me, I would never have lifted my spear against them. They have brought this on themselves. 3 But now tell me why you have fled from them and have come over to us. In any event, you have come to safety. Take courage! You will live tonight and ever after. 4 No one will hurt you. Rather, all will treat you well, as they do the servants of my Lord King Nebuchadnezzar."

5 Judith answered him, "Accept the words of your slave, and let your servant speak in your presence. I will say nothing false to my Lord this night. 6 If you follow out the words of your servant, God will accomplish something through you, and my Lord will not fail to achieve his purposes. 7 By the life of Nebuchadnezzar, king of the whole earth, and by the power of him who has sent you to direct every living being! Not only do human beings serve him because of you, but also the animals of the field and the cattle and the birds of the air will live, because of your power, under Nebuchadnezzar and all his house. 8 For we have heard of your wisdom and skill, and it is reported throughout the whole world that you alone are the best in the whole kingdom, the most informed and the most astounding in military strategy.

9 "Now as for Achior's speech in your council, we have heard his words, for the people of Bethulia spared him and he told them all he had said to you. 10 Therefore, Lord and master, do not disregard what he said, but keep it in your mind, for it is true. Indeed our nation cannot be punished, nor can the sword prevail against them, unless they sin against their God.

11 "But now, in order that my Lord may not be defeated and his purpose frustrated, death will fall upon them, for a sin has overtaken them by which they are about to provoke their God to anger when they do what is wrong. 12 Since their food supply is exhausted and their water has almost given out, they have planned to kill their livestock and have determined to use all that God by his laws has forbidden them to eat. 13 They have decided to consume the first fruits of the grain and the tithes of the wine and oil, which they had consecrated and set aside for the priests who minister in the pres-

ence of our God in Jerusalem—things it is not lawful for any of the people even to touch with their hands. 14 Since even the people in Jerusalem have been doing this, they have sent messengers there in order to bring back permission from the council of the elders. 15 When the response reaches them and they act upon it, on that very day they will be handed over to you to be destroyed.

16 "So when I, your slave, learned all this, I fled from them. God has sent me to accomplish with you things that will astonish the whole world wherever people shall hear about them. 17 Your servant is indeed God-fearing and serves the God of heaven night and day. So, my Lord, I will remain with you; but every night your servant will go out into the valley and pray to God. He will tell me when they have committed their sins. 18 Then I will come and tell you, so that you may go out with your whole army, and not one of them will be able to withstand you. 19 Then I will lead you through Judea, until you come to Jerusalem; there I will set your throne. You will drive them like sheep that have no shepherd, and no dog will so much as growl at you. For this was told me to give me foreknowledge; it was announced to me, and I was sent to tell you."

20 Her words pleased Holofernes and all his servants. They marveled at her wisdom and said, 21 "No other woman from one end of the earth to the other looks so beautiful or speaks so wisely!" 22 Then Holofernes said to her, "God has done well to send you ahead of the people, to strengthen our hands and bring destruction on those who have despised my Lord. 23 You are not only beautiful in appearance, but wise in speech. If you do as you have said, your God shall be my God, and you shall live in the palace of King Nebuchadnezzar and be renowned throughout the whole world."

12 Then he commanded them to bring her in where his silver dinnerware was kept, and ordered them to set a table for her with some of his own delicacies, and with some of his own wine to drink. 2 But Judith said, "I cannot partake of them, or it will be an offense; but I will have enough with the things I brought with me."

3 Holofernes said to her, "If your supply runs out, where can we get you more of the same? For none of your people are here with us." 4 Judith replied, "As surely as you live, my Lord, your servant will not use up the supplies I have with me before the Lord carries out by my hand what he has determined."

5 Then the servants of Holofernes brought her into the tent, and she slept until midnight. Toward the morning watch she got up 6 and sent this message to Holofernes: "Let my Lord now give orders to allow your servant to go out and pray." 7 So Holofernes commanded his guards not to hinder her. She remained in the camp three days. She went out each night to the valley of Bethulia, and bathed at the spring in the camp. 8 After bathing, she prayed the Lord God of Israel to direct her way for the triumph of his people. 9 Then she returned purified and stayed in the tent until she ate her food toward evening.

10 On the fourth day Holofernes held a banquet for his personal attendants only, and did not invite any of his officers. 11 He said to Bagoas, the eunuch who had charge of his personal affairs, "Go and persuade the Hebrew woman who is in your care to join us and to eat and drink with us. 12 For it would be a disgrace if we let such a woman go without having intercourse with her. If we do not seduce her, she will laugh at us."

13 So Bagoas left the presence of Holofernes, and approached her and said, "Let this pretty girl not hesitate to come to my Lord to be honored in his presence, and to enjoy drinking wine with us, and to become today like one of the Assyrian women who serve in the palace of Nebuchadnezzar." 14 Judith replied, "Who am I to refuse my Lord? Whatever pleases him I will do at once, and it will be a joy to me until the day of my death." 15 So she proceeded to dress herself in all her woman's finery. Her maid went ahead and spread for her on the ground before Holofernes the lambskins she had received from Bagoas for her daily use in reclining.

16 Then Judith came in and lay down. Holofernes' heart was ravished with her and his passion was aroused, for he had been waiting for an opportunity to seduce her from the day he first saw her. 17 So Holofernes said to her, "Have a drink and be merry with us!" 18 Judith said, "I will gladly drink, my Lord, because today is the greatest day in my whole life." 19 Then she took what her maid had prepared and ate and drank before him. 20 Holofernes was greatly pleased with her, and drank a great quantity of wine, much more than he had ever drunk in any one day since he was born.

13 When evening came, his slaves quickly withdrew. Bagoas closed the tent from outside and shut out the attendants from his master's presence. They went to bed, for they all were weary because the banquet had lasted so long. 2 But Judith was left alone in the tent, with Holofernes stretched out on his bed, for he was dead drunk. 3 Now Judith had told her maid to stand outside the bedchamber and to wait for her to come out, as she did on the other days;

Cristoforo Allori (1577–1621): The servant looks anxiously at her mistress, but Judith holds the head of Holofernes calmly in her hand, showing neither emotion nor weakness.
Galleria Pitti, Florence

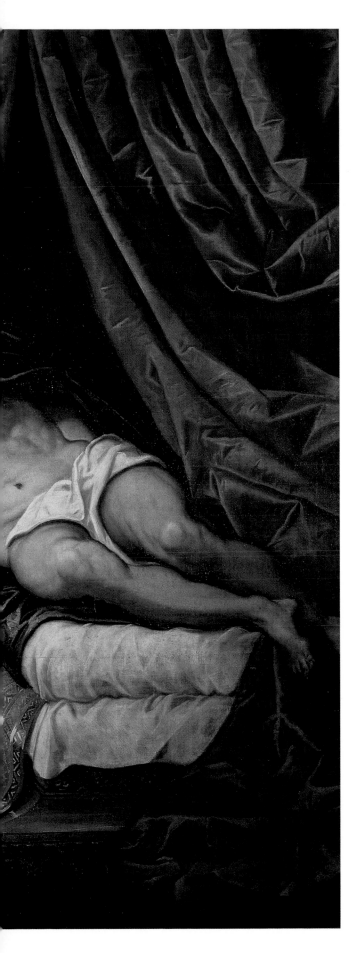

for she said she would be going out for her prayers. She had said the same thing to Bagoas. [4] So everyone went out, and no one, either small or great, was left in the bedchamber. Then Judith, standing beside his bed, said in her heart, "O Lord God of all might, look in this hour on the work of my hands for the exaltation of Jerusalem. [5] Now indeed is the time to help your heritage and to carry out my design to destroy the enemies who have risen up against us."

[6] She went up to the bedpost near Holofernes' head, and took down his sword that hung there. [7] She came close to his bed, took hold of the hair of his head, and said, "Give me strength today, O Lord God of Israel!" [8] Then she struck his neck twice with all her might, and cut off his head. [9] Next she rolled his body off the bed and pulled down the canopy from the posts. Soon afterward she went out and gave Holofernes' head to her maid, [10] who placed it in her food bag. Then the two of them went out together, as they were accustomed to do for prayer. They passed through the camp, circled around the valley, and went up the mountain to Bethulia, and came to its gates. [11] From a distance Judith called out to the sentries at the gates, "Open, open the gate! God, our God, is with us, still showing his power in Israel and his strength against our enemies, as he has done today!"

[12] When the people of her town heard her voice, they hurried down to the town gate and summoned the elders of the town. [13] They all ran together, both small and great, for it seemed unbelievable that she had returned. They opened the gate and welcomed them. Then they lit a fire to give light, and gathered around them. [14] Then she said to them with a loud voice, "Praise God, O praise him! Praise God, who has not withdrawn his mercy from the house of Israel, but has destroyed our enemies by my hand this very night!"

[15] Then she pulled the head out of the bag and showed it to them, and said, "See here, the head of Holofernes the commander of the Assyrian army, and here is the canopy beneath which he lay in his drunken stupor. The Lord has struck him down by the hand of a woman. [16] As the Lord lives, who has protected me in the way I went, I swear that it was

Tintoretto (1518–1594): Turning her head away, Judith covers the mutilated body of Holofernes. The maidservant, kneeling on the floor with the head next to her, looks timidly once more at the dead man.
Museo del Prado, Madrid

my face that seduced him to his destruction, and that he committed no sin with me, to defile and shame me."

¹⁷ All the people were greatly astonished. They bowed down and worshiped God, and said with one accord, "Blessed are you our God, who have this day humiliated the enemies of your people."
¹⁸ Then Uzziah said to her, "O daughter, you are blessed by the Most High God above all other women on earth; and blessed be the Lord God, who created the heavens and the earth, who has guided you to cut off the head of the leader of our enemies. ¹⁹ Your praise will never depart from the hearts of those who remember the power of God. ²⁰ May God grant this to be a perpetual honor to you, and may he reward you with blessings, because you risked your own life when our nation was brought low, and you averted our ruin, walking in the straight path before our God." And all the people said, "Amen. Amen."

The following two chapters report how Judith addresses her people and summons them to attack the enemies. At first, the Assyrians meet the Israelites with contempt. But when they discover that their general lies dead in his tent, they lose courage and scatter in all directions; many are killed by the pursuing Jews. Judith's heroic exploit is universally acclaimed.

T hen she said to them with a loud voice,
"Praise God, O praise him!
Praise God, who has not withdrawn his mercy
from the house of Israel, but has destroyed our
enemies by my hand this very night!"

Judith 13:14

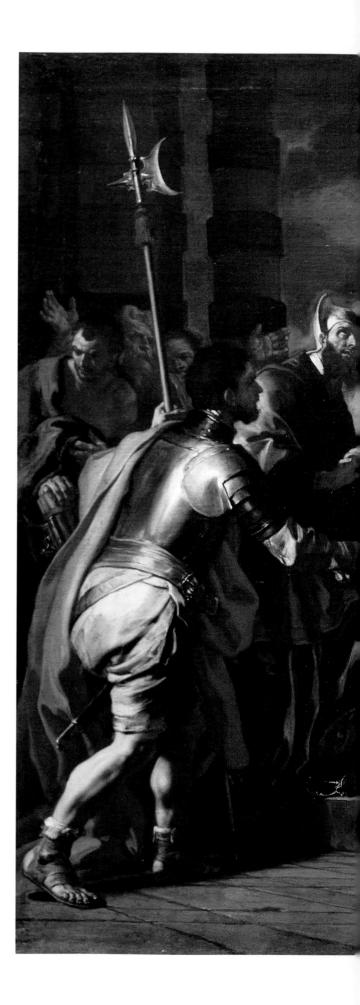

Francesco Solimena (1657–1747), master of the late Neapolitan baroque, shows Judith producing the head of the enemy general to the frightened citizens of the besieged town of Bethulia to fortify their courage. She stands aloft, like a goddess of victory, surrounded by angels.
Kunsthistorisches Museum, Vienna

"No one ever again spread terror among the Israelites during the lifetime of Judith"

Dorothee Soelle

In the Bible, there is a tradition of strong and courageous heroines, which contradicts clichés of female weakness and timidity. During the time of occupying the Promised Land and founding a state, prophetesses and judges such as Deborah appear; and then there is Jael, the callous heroine who slays her sleeping enemy (Judges 5). But only in the postexilic period when there is no longer a state of Israel, we have Esther and Judith, who become the rescuers of their people. The apocryphal story of Judith and Holofernes surely offers the most vivid image of this new type of woman. No other woman in biblical tradition has been so honored as Judith was with the statement that "no fear was in Israel when Judith was alive."

The connection between war and rape, the mass defilement of women of the defeated nation by the victors, has existed for thousands of years. The prospect of having women to rape, often to death, is an incentive to fight better. A reversal of this ancient pattern, in which woman becomes the active agent and man the victim, will therefore often seem unacceptable. Though war and lust

may be combined—as the German word Kriegs-Lust suggests—as long, as the men are the winners on both counts, this is not true for lust and murder when, as in Judith's story, a woman utilizes lust in the interest of her people.

But the Bible does not share these conflicting feelings. It does not object to Judith; she is one of those highly respected widows who later became the model community leaders in the early Christian church. In the medieval Bibles for the poor, Judith, together with Eve, Pharaoh's daughter, Rebekah, Tamar, Bathsheba and Susanna, becomes allegorically linked to Christ. Her wisdom, which inspires confidence, is extolled.

Her story takes place at the time of King Nebuchadnezzar; next to him, his general Holofernes, Judith's antagonist, fades. Holofernes is warned by Achior, the Ammonite, against the spirit and the God of the Hebrews. Yet he dares to besiege the Jewish town of Bethulia and to cut off its water supply. The widow Judith, distinguished by her beauty, virtue, intelligence and piety, leaves the besieged town and enters the enemy camp under the pretext of betraying the Jews to Holofernes. Accompanied by her maidservant, she stays for three days and nights, but touches none of the enemy's food. She charms Holofernes and, beautifully dressed, accepts his invitation to a banquet. Late at night, the servants and Judith's maid are sent away and she is alone with the drunken general who already sees his wishes fulfilled. She kills him with his own sword. His head is hidden in a bag and smuggled out of the camp. She shows it to the discouraged Jews, who now easily scatter their enemies.

This bloody story at first meant little to me; it seemed to me overloaded with pious sentiments and charged which a strange notion of heroism. But my displeasure disappeared when I heard a contemporary story that seemed to breathe the same spirit. In Nicaragua, under the dictator Somoza, a woman in the liberation movement performed an analogous deed in the 1970s. General Vega, a member of the tyrant's ruling party and an infamous torturer for the secret service, had cast his eye on a beautiful lawyer, Nora Astorga, and tried to seduce her. One day she let him know by phone that she was ready

to cooperate and he should prepare to receive her. Her plan was to capture the drunken general with the help of resistance fighters and to exchange him for imprisoned freedom fighters. But her lover, refusing all preliminaries such as cognac or other refreshment, flung himself upon the woman as she entered, dragged her upon the bed, and left her no choice but to alarm the hidden guerillas. In the ensuing shooting, the general was killed.

Later, after the Sandinistas were in power and Nora Astorga was to become Nicaragua's ambassador in Washington, this story was published by the media. This modern Judith was morally condemned and was never endorsed. She later worked as ambassador for her country at the United Nations until her early death in 1988.

This Judith, too, subordinated her personal concerns to the liberation of her people. She, too, used her sexual appeal as a weapon. She, too, demonstrated strategic wisdom, determination, and courage. As it was said of Judith that "there was no fear in Israel as long as Judith was alive," one can probably say of this unusual Central American woman that, for a short while, she diminished the fear of the poor people in her country.

Left: This bronze (originally gold-plated) statue of Judith, about to decapitate Holofernes, was created by Donatello (1386–1466) as the centerpiece of a well, between 1456 and 1460. It now stands next to Michelangelo's David on the Piazza della Signoria in Florence. In 1495, the following inscription was added on the baser: Exemplum publicae salutis (An exemplary deed for the common good).

Opposite: Holding the sword with which she decapitated Holofernes in her hand, Judith and her servant, who is carrying the head of the murdered man in a basket on her hip, are looking back once more to the tent where the deed was accomplished. Judith's face shows consternation rather than triumph. This painting, with its almost three-dimensional figures, is by Artemisia Gentileschi (1597–ca. 1652). Born in Rome, Gentileschi worked for a while with his father Orazio at the English court of Charles I and later mostly in Naples. Galleria Palatina, Florence

Ancient and medieval sources

Joe H. Kirchberger

The first seven chapters of Judith record how Nebuchadnezzar, king of Assyria, defeated the mighty Arphaxad, king of the Medes, and thereafter thought of himself as lord of the world. He sent envoys to all parts of the world, to Samaria and Jerusalem, to Goshen or Egypt, and "to the borders of the black peoples," asking for submission. But all the nations sent the envoys back ignominiously. So Nebuchadnezzar decided on a campaign of revenge and ordered his general Holofernes to move against all western countries and to subjugate them. Holofernes crossed the Euphrates, invaded Damascus and Mesopotamia, burned all crops, and had trees and vineyards cut down. Then many of the princes, including those of Libya, Syria, and Mesopotamia, surrendered. The children of Israel were also seized by fear but, encouraged by their priest Joakim, took up arms to resist. When Holofernes heard this, he asked his colonels who these Israelites were, and Achior, head of the Ammonites, answered him, telling him of the exodus from Egypt and the conquest of the land of Canaan, adding that the children of Israel had always been victorious as long as they obeyed their God. This enraged Holofernes and his colonels. Achior was tied to a tree and Holofernes vowed

to punish him as soon as he had defeated the Israelites. But the Jews freed Achior and took him to the town of Bethulia where he told them his story. Uzziah, the commander in Bethulia, retreated into the mountains and Holofernes began the siege of the town. On the advice of the Ammonites and Moabites, he had the town's water supply cut off. Shortly the besieged were suffering horribly from lack of water; they repented for having sinned against God and prayed to him to punish them but not to let them fall into the hands of the enemy. Uzziah said to them: "Let us hold out for five days more; by that time the Lord our God will turn his mercy to us again. . . . If . . . no help comes for us, I will do as you say."

JEWISH TRADITION does not add much to the elaborate narrative in the book of Judith. An apocryphal text, it was not considered a part of the Hebrew Bible. But tradition has it that Holofernes surrendered his sword to Judith in the course of the meal, saying: "Before you, I am helpless." Further, it is claimed that there was no fear in Israel as long as Judith was alive, and, indeed, long after her death. Josephus does not mention Judith at all.

YET ALREADY in the early Middle Ages, the Judith story was retold in Germanic poetry. There is an Old English epic of the early tenth century, and in the so-called Vorauer Manuscript, named after an important copyist center in Styria, there exists an early Judith text of the twelfth century and another later thirteenth-century version. In these poems, Judith is the central figure. Holofernes is merely an object, the hated enemy and Judith's victim. The older poem is written in a popular ballad style, the later and longer text is apparently by a clergyman from Lower Austria and confines itself to retelling the biblical story in a simple, often clumsy manner. Neither of the two German poems develops any profound insights or religious ideas.

Dante mentions the death of Holofernes in the twelfth canto of his *Purgatorio*, but Judith herself does not appear.

They marveled at her beauty and admired the Israelites, judging them by her.

They said to one another, "Who can despise these people, who have women like this among them?

It is not wise to leave one of their men alive, for if we let them go they will be able to beguile

the whole world!"

Judith 10:19

*Above: Judith, having returned to Bethulia, pulls Holo-
fernes' head from her bag and shows it to the people to
fill the frightened crowd with courage. "See here, the head
of Holofernes, the commander of the Assyrian army. . . .
The Lord has struck him down by the hand of a woman."
Illustration from the* Codex hebr. 37, fol. 81 b r, 1428.
Staats- und Universitätsbibliothek, Hamburg

*Opposite: Judith is brought to the tent of Holofernes,
who assures her of his affection and clemency. Illustration
from the* Codex hebr. 37, fol. 80v, 1428.
Staats- und Universitätsbibliothek, Hamburg

Esther

THE REQUEST OF A QUEEN

Esther
Chapter 1, verses 1–4; Chapter 2, verses 1–23
Chapter 4, verses 1–17; Chapter 5, verses 1–14
Chapter 6, verses 1–14; Chapter 7, verses 1–10
Chapter 8, verses 1–14

Esther's story is set in the city of Babylon at the time of the exile, although according to historical records King Ahasuerus (Xerxes) did not ascend the throne until 486 B.C., long after the exile. (On the other hand, the character described here corresponds approximately with that of Xerxes as we know him from Herodotus, the Greek historian and younger contemporary of the Persian king.) Historians have disputed the likelihood of a mass pogrom of the Jews supposedly ordered by the Achaemenid dynasty well known for its tolerance, and found even less believable the claim that it ordered later the extermination of fifteen thousand of its own subjects, and that they accepted their fate without resistance. It is known, further, that the name of Xerxes' wife was Amestris, leaving no room for a Vashti or Esther. Some have attempted to interpret the names mentioned in the book symbolically. A possible derivation of Esther's name from that of the Babylonian goddess Ishtar seems fairly obvious, and a similar connection has been made between the names Mordecai and Marduk. It is strange, however, that the book of Esther, alone among all the books of the Bible, never mentions God's name.

This happened in the days of Ahasuerus, the same Ahasuerus who ruled over one hundred twenty-seven provinces from India to Ethiopia. ² In those days when King Ahasuerus sat on his royal throne in the citadel of Susa, ³ in the third year of his reign, he gave a banquet for all his officials and ministers. The army of Persia and Media and the nobles and governors of the provinces were present, ⁴ while he displayed the great wealth of his kingdom and the splendor and pomp of his majesty for many days, one hundred eighty days in all.

There follows a report of a large, luxurious feast given by the king in his palace while his queen, beautiful Vashti, celebrates her own festival with the women of the palace. On the seventh day, King Ahasuerus orders the queen to be brought before him so that he may show her beauty to his guests and noblemen. She refuses to appear. The king is infuriated, particularly because Vashti is setting a bad example for disobedient wives, and expels her.

2 After these things, when the anger of King Ahasuerus had abated, he remembered Vashti and what she had done and what had been decreed against her. ² Then the king's servants who attended him said, "Let beautiful young virgins be sought out for the king. ³ And let the king appoint commissioners in all the provinces of his kingdom to gather all the beautiful young virgins to the harem in the citadel of Susa under custody of Hegai, the king's eunuch, who is in charge of the women; let their cosmetic treatments be given them. ⁴ And let the girl who pleases the king be queen instead of Vashti." This pleased the king, and he did so. ⁵ Now there was a Jew in the citadel of Susa whose name was Mordecai son of Jair son of Shimei son of Kish, a Benjaminite. ⁶ Kish had been carried away from Jerusalem among the captives carried away with King Jeconiah of Judah, whom King Nebuchadnezzar of Babylon had carried away. ⁷ Mordecai had brought up Hadassah, that is Esther, his cousin, for she had neither father nor mother; the girl was fair and beautiful, and when her father and her mother died, Mordecai adopted her as his own daughter.

⁸ So when the king's order and his edict were proclaimed, and when many young women were gathered in the citadel of Susa in custody of Hegai, Esther also was taken into the king's palace and put in custody of Hegai, who had charge of the women. ⁹ The girl pleased him and won his favor, and he quickly provided her with her cosmetic treatments

Andrea del Castagno (ca. 1420–1457) painted
Queen Esther as a self-assured, beautiful woman,
dressed in the style of the early Renaissance.
Galleria degli Uffizi, Florence

and her portion of food, and with seven chosen maids from the king's palace, and advanced her and her maids to the best place in the harem. ¹⁰ Esther did not reveal her people or kindred, for Mordecai had charged her not to tell. ¹¹ Every day Mordecai would walk around in front of the court of the harem, to learn how Esther was and how she fared.

¹² The turn came for each girl to go in to King Ahasuerus, after being twelve months under the regulations for the women, since this was the regular period of their cosmetic treatment, six months with oil of myrrh and six months with perfumes and cosmetics for women. ¹³ When the girl went in to the king she was given whatever she asked for to take with her from the harem to the king's palace. ¹⁴ In the evening she went in; then in the morning she came back to the second harem in custody of Shaashgaz, the king's eunuch, who was in charge of the concubines; she did not go in to the king again, unless the king delighted in her and she was summoned by name.

¹⁵ When the turn came for Esther daughter of Abihail the uncle of Mordecai, who had adopted her as his own daughter, to go in to the king, she asked for nothing except what Hegai the king's eunuch, who had charge of the women, advised. Now Esther was admired by all who saw her. ¹⁶ When Esther was taken to King Ahasuerus in his royal palace in the tenth month, which is the month of Tebeth, in the seventh year of his reign, ¹⁷ the king loved Esther more than all the other women; of all the virgins she won his favor and devotion, so that he set the royal crown on her head and made her queen instead of Vashti. ¹⁸ Then the king gave a great banquet to all his officials and ministers—"Esther's banquet." He also granted a holiday to the provinces, and gave gifts with royal liberality.

¹⁹ When the virgins were being gathered together, Mordecai was sitting at the king's gate. ²⁰ Now Esther had not revealed her kindred or her people, as Mordecai had charged her; for Esther obeyed Mordecai just as when she was brought up by him. ²¹ In those days, while Mordecai was sitting at the king's gate, Bigthan and Teresh, two of the king's eunuchs, who guarded the threshold, became angry and conspired to assassinate King Ahasuerus. ²² But the matter came to the knowledge of Mordecai, and he told it to Queen Esther, and Esther told the king in the name of Mordecai. ²³ When the affair was investigated and found to be so, both the men were hanged on the gallows. It was recorded in the book of the annals in the presence of the king.

In the following chapter we are told that Haman the Agagite was raised above all princes by Ahasuerus. They were required to bend their knees before him, but Mordecai refused to do so. Haman was seized by such hatred and fury that he purposed to destroy not only Mordecai but the whole Jewish community in the empire. He persuaded the king to make known such orders all over the empire.

4 When Mordecai learned all that had been done, Mordecai tore his clothes and put on sackcloth and ashes, and went through the city, wailing with a loud and bitter cry; ² he went up to the entrance of the king's gate, for no one might enter the king's gate clothed with sackcloth. ³ In every province, wherever the king's command and his decree came, there was great mourning among the Jews, with fasting and weeping and lamenting, and most of them lay in sackcloth and ashes.

⁴ When Esther's maids and her eunuchs came and told her, the queen was deeply distressed; she sent garments to clothe Mordecai, so that he might take off his sackcloth; but he would not accept them. ⁵ Then Esther called for Hathach, one of the king's eunuchs, who had been appointed to attend her, and ordered him to go to Mordecai to learn what was happening and why. ⁶ Hathach went out to Mordecai in the open square of the city in front of the king's gate, ⁷ and Mordecai told him all that had happened to him, and the exact sum of money that Haman had promised to pay into the king's treasuries for the destruction of the Jews. ⁸ Mordecai also gave him a copy of the written decree issued in Susa for their destruction, that he might show it to Esther, explain it to her, and charge her to go to the king to make supplication to him and entreat him for her people.

⁹ Hathach went and told Esther what Mordecai had said. ¹⁰ Then Esther spoke to Hathach and gave him a message for Mordecai, saying, ¹¹ "All the king's servants and the people of the king's provinces know that if any man or woman goes to the king inside the inner court without being called, there is but one law—all alike are to be

Opposite: Esther, as every virgin to be presented to King Ahasuerus, has first to undergo cosmetic treatment for one year; she was beautified with balsam and myrrh for six months, and with aromatic spices for another six months. Painting by Theodore Chassériau (1819–1856), a disciple of Ingres (1842).
Musée du Louvre, Paris

Esther on her way to King Ahasuerus. Mordecai, her relative who had adopted her after the death of her parents, has sent her two messages imploring her to plead with the king not to deliver the Jews to ruthless Haman. Painting by Filippino Lippi (1457–1504), a student of Botticelli. National Gallery of Canada, Ottawa

put to death. Only if the king holds out the golden scepter to someone, may that person live. I myself have not been called to come in to the king for thirty days." ¹² When they told Mordecai what Esther had said, ¹³ Mordecai told them to reply to Esther, "Do not think that in the king's palace you will escape any more than all the other Jews. ¹⁴ For if you keep silence at such a time as this, relief and deliverance will rise for the Jews from another quarter, but you and your father's family will perish. Who knows? Perhaps you have come to royal dignity for just such a time as this." ¹⁵ Then Esther said in reply to Mordecai, ¹⁶ "Go, gather all the Jews to be found in Susa, and hold a fast on my behalf, and neither eat nor drink for three days, night or day. I and my maids will also fast as you do. After that I will go to the king, though it is against the law; and if I perish, I perish." ¹⁷ Mordecai then went away and did everything as Esther had ordered him.

5 On the third day Esther put on her royal robes and stood in the inner court of the king's palace, opposite the king's hall. The king was sitting on his royal throne inside the palace opposite the entrance to the palace. ² As soon as the king saw Queen Esther standing in the court, she won his favor and he held out to her the golden scepter that was in his hand. Then Esther approached and touched the top of the scepter. ³ The king said to her, "What is it, Queen Esther? What is your request? It shall be given you, even to the half of my kingdom." ⁴ Then Esther said, "If it pleases the king, let the king and Haman come today to a banquet that I have prepared for the king." ⁵ Then the king said, "Bring Haman quickly, so that we may do as Esther desires." So the king and Haman came to the banquet that Esther had prepared. ⁶ While they were drinking wine, the king said to Esther, "What is your petition? It shall be granted you. And what is your request? Even to the half of my kingdom, it shall be fulfilled." ⁷ Then Esther said, "This is my petition and request: ⁸ If I have won the king's favor, and if it pleases the king to grant my petition and fulfill my request, let the king and Haman come tomorrow to the banquet that I will prepare for them, and then I will do as the king has said."

⁹ Haman went out that day happy and in good spirits. But when Haman saw Mordecai in the king's gate, and observed that he neither rose nor trembled before him, he was infuriated with Mordecai; ¹⁰ nevertheless Haman restrained himself and went home. Then he sent and called for his friends and his wife Zeresh, ¹¹ and Haman recounted to them the splendor of his riches, the number of his sons, all the promotions with which the king had honored him, and how he had advanced him above the officials and the ministers of the king. ¹² Haman added, "Even Queen Esther let no one but myself come with the king to the banquet that she prepared. Tomorrow also I am invited by her, together with the king. ¹³ Yet all this does me no good so long as I see the Jew Mordecai sitting at the king's gate." ¹⁴ Then his wife Zeresh and all his friends said to him, "Let a gallows fifty cubits high be made, and in the morning tell the king to have Mordecai hanged on it; then go with the king to the banquet in good spirits." This advice pleased Haman, and he had the gallows made.

6 On that night the king could not sleep, and he gave orders to bring the book of records, the annals, and they were read to the king. ² It was found written how Mordecai had told about Bigthana and Teresh, two of the king's eunuchs, who guarded the threshold, and who had conspired to assassinate King Ahasuerus. ³ Then the king said, "What honor or distinction has been bestowed on Mordecai for this?" The king's servants who attended him said, "Nothing has been done for him." ⁴ The king said, "Who is in the court?" Now Haman had just entered the outer court of the king's palace to speak to the king about having Mordecai hanged on the gallows that he had prepared for him. ⁵ So the king's servants told him, "Haman is there, standing in the court." The king said, "Let him come in." ⁶ So Haman came in, and the king said to him, "What shall be done for the man whom the king wishes to honor?" Haman said to himself, "Whom would the king wish to honor more than me?" ⁷ So Haman said to the king, "For the man whom the king wishes to honor, ⁸ let royal robes be brought, which the king has worn, and a horse that the king has ridden, with a royal crown on its head. ⁹ Let the robes and the horse be handed over to one of the king's most noble officials; let him robe the man whom the king wishes to honor, and let him conduct the man on horseback through the open square of the city, proclaiming before him: 'Thus shall it be done for the man whom the king wishes to honor.'" ¹⁰ Then the king said to Haman, "Quickly, take the robes and the horse, as you have said, and do so to the Jew Mordecai who sits at the king's gate. Leave out nothing that you have mentioned." ¹¹ So Haman took the robes and the horse and robed Mordecai and led him riding through the open square of the city, proclaiming, "Thus shall it be done for the man whom the king wishes to honor."

Above: Esther, resolved to help her fellow Jews, has approached the king, but her strength leaves her and she collapses in a faint; the king is touched and comforts her. Painting by Antoine Coypel (1661–1722). Musée du Louvre, Paris

Left: Inside a richly decorated initial letter from a manuscript at the Florentine Museum of the Cathedral, Queen Esther sits on a thronelike armchair, a banderole in her hands. Museo dell'Opera del Duomo, Florence

Pages 104/105: The Dutch painter Herri met de Bles (ca. 1500–1559/60) has depicted on the center panel of a triptych Queen Esther kneeling before the king to ask for mercy for her Jewish fellow believers. The two side panels show the banquet the king holds for Esther, and that which Esther holds for the king and Haman. Pinacoteca Nazionale, Bologna

¹² Then Mordecai returned to the king's gate, but Haman hurried to his house, mourning and with his head covered. ¹³ When Haman told his wife Zeresh and all his friends everything that had happened to him, his advisers and his wife Zeresh said to him, "If Mordecai, before whom your downfall has begun, is of the Jewish people, you will not prevail against him, but will surely fall before him." ¹⁴ "While they were still talking with him, the king's eunuchs arrived and hurried Haman off to the banquet that Esther had prepared.

7 So the king and Haman went in to feast with Queen Esther. ² On the second day, as they were drinking wine, the king again said to Esther, "What is your petition, Queen Esther? It shall be granted you. And what is your request? Even to the half of my kingdom, it shall be fulfilled."

³ Then Queen Esther answered, "If I have won your favor, O king, and if it pleases the king, let my life be given me—that is my petition—and the lives of my people—that is my request. ⁴ For we have been sold, I and my people, to be destroyed, to be killed, and to be annihilated. If we had been sold merely as slaves, men and women, I would have held my peace; but no enemy can compensate for this damage to the king." ⁵ Then King Ahasuerus said to Queen Esther, "Who is he, and where is he, who has presumed to do this?" ⁶ Esther said, "A foe and enemy, this wicked Haman!" Then Haman was terrified before the king and the queen. ⁷ The king rose from the feast in wrath and went into the palace garden, but Haman stayed to beg his life from Queen Esther, for he saw that the king had determined to destroy him. ⁸ When the king returned from the palace garden to the banquet hall, Haman had thrown himself on the couch where Esther was reclining; and the king said, "Will he even assault the queen in my presence, in my own house?" As the words left the mouth of the king, they covered Haman's face. ⁹ Then Harbona, one of the eunuchs in attendance on the king, said, "Look, the very gallows that Haman has prepared for Mordecai, whose word saved the king, stands at Haman's house, fifty cubits high." And the king said, "Hang him on that." ¹⁰ "So they hanged Haman on the gallows that he had prepared for Mordecai. Then the anger of the king abated.

8 On that day King Ahasuerus gave to Queen Esther the house of Haman, the enemy of the Jews; and Mordecai came before the king, for Esther had told what he was to her. ² Then the king took off his signet ring, which he had taken from Haman, and gave it to Mordecai. So Esther set Mordecai over the house of Haman. ³ Then Esther spoke again to the king; she fell at his feet, weeping and pleading with him to avert the evil design of Haman the Agagite and the plot that he had devised against the Jews. ⁴ The king held out the golden scepter to Esther, ⁵ and Esther rose and stood before the king. She said, "If it pleases the king, and if I have won his favor, and if the thing seems right before the king, and I have his approval, let an order be written to revoke the letters devised by Haman son of Hammedatha the Agagite, which he wrote giving orders to destroy the Jews who are in all the provinces of the king. ⁶ For how can I bear to see the calamity that is coming on my people? Or how can I bear to see the destruction of my kindred?" ⁷ Then King Ahasuerus said to Queen Esther and to the Jew Mordecai, "See, I have given Esther the house of Haman, and they have hanged him on the gallows, because he plotted to lay hands on the Jews. ⁸ You may write as you please with regard to the Jews, in the name of the king, and seal it with the king's ring; for an edict written in the name of the king and sealed with the king's ring cannot be revoked. ⁹ The king's secretaries were summoned at that time, in the third month, which is the month of Sivan, on the twenty-third day; and an edict was written, according to all that Mordecai commanded, to the Jews and to the satraps and the governors and the officials of the provinces from India to Ethiopia, one hundred twenty-seven provinces, to every province in its own script and to every people in its own language, and also to the Jews in their script and their language. ¹⁰ He wrote letters in the name of King Ahasuerus, sealed them with the king's ring, and sent them by mounted couriers riding on fast steeds bred from the royal herd. ¹¹ By these letters the king allowed the Jews who were in every city to assemble and defend their lives, to destroy, to kill, and to annihilate any armed force of any people or province that might attack them, with their children and women, and to plunder their goods ¹² on a single day throughout all the provinces of King Ahasuerus, on the thirteenth day of the twelfth month, which is the month of Adar. ¹³ A copy of the writ was to be issued as a decree in every province and published to all peoples, and the Jews were to be ready on that day to take revenge on their enemies. ¹⁴ So the couriers, mounted on their swift royal steeds, hurried out, urged by the king's command. The decree was issued in the citadel of Susa.

At the sight of Haman's gallows

Dorothee Soelle

The figures of two women emerge in the book of Esther, Vashti and Esther. Both play their parts in the hidden history of strength against superior power and routine coercion, but only one is shown in the bright light of the biblical narrative; the other woman, Vashti, disappears at the outset, after a courageous act of resistance.

The short historical novel for which we have to take the book of Esther is set in the time of Xerxes (486–465 B.C.). The Persian Empire is still at the peak of its power. Splendor, wealth, and luxury are described in the fantastic festivals at the beginning of the book. The king and his chosen guests engage in a contest concerning who possesses the most beautiful woman, a quarrel among drunks, the talk of vulgar men in a saloon. King Ahasuerus is quite sure of himself and orders his seven chamberlains to fetch his wife "to show the peoples and the officials her beauty" (Esther 1:11). Vashti refuses to obey. It is not recorded why she rejects this proposal, but presumably she was expected to pose in the nude before the guests, as in Herodotus's famous story of Gyges and Kandaules. The exhibited object is to be appraised uncovered. When Vashti, the aristocrat, refuses, the king becomes furious. An official response is called for. Is this not a threat to the whole social order? More wives might be tempted to question the right of possession! The queen loses her throne and all privileges, and above all this little incident is used by the leading lawyers as a pretext for an order designed to secure the rule of the husband in his house. The inconspicuous act of noncooperation and resistance against the all-powerful patriarchal structure has unleashed deep anxieties and prompted legal machinations.

At the same time, the Vashti episode opens the door for the story of the Jewess Esther. The rebellious queen must be replaced, and perhaps the

Paolo Veronese (1538–1588) has again painted Esther before the king. But here Esther is accompanied by maidservants, and the action takes place in a multistoried room, with spectators looking down from its gallery.
Gallelria degli Uffizi, Florence

narrator has transferred a certain amount of sympathy for courageous Vashti—who now disappears from the scene—to Esther. At least the basic theme, the contrast between patriarchal power and female fragility, is developed in the stories of both women.

Esther is a poor orphan who grows up with her uncle and foster father Mordecai. The story is told, not without humor, how the most beautiful virgins from all the provinces are sent to the king's harem

With God's benediction Esther is crowned queen. Ornamental initial letter from a Bible manuscript at Barcelona.

to be subjected to a one-year cosmetic preparation by means of myrrh, balsam, and asses' milk. The Jewish girl Esther whose name may mean "to hide" (which would hint at her personal situation as well as the fate of her people), is chosen as the queen. Upon the advice of the experienced Mordecai, who has a position at the court, she must conceal her Judaism. But she does reveal to the king a conspiracy against him, not without mentioning her guardian Mordecai.

A counterpoint to this fairy tale develops through another courtier, Haman, who has worked his way up and is now raised above the other public servants. Following Persian custom he demands homage on bended knees, which, however, the Jew Mordecai refuses. This slight makes Haman a persecutor of all Jews. Tradition found this explanation for his hatred of all things Jewish too meager, and searched for other reasons to explain Haman's anti-Semitism, asking one of those unanswered

questions that Nelly Sachs, in our century, formulated thus: "Why this black hatred to the simple fact that you exist, Israel?" The biblical Haman is the symbol for this black answer, the blind and totalitarian determination to destroy the Jewish people. Avarice and jealousy may have played a part in it, but the most profound reason for what in modern times is called anti-Semitism is the otherness of the Jews; they are guided by laws and rules other than those of the "peoples." The word "God" is never spoken in the book of Esther, yet it is this holding on to a different God that made this people different, separate, and the target of irrational hatred.

Now minister Haman has a precise and thorough plan of genocide of the Jews. His symbol is the huge gallows set up on the palace grounds. King Xerxes, who in this whole book appears to be a mere puppet with crown and scepter, agrees to Haman's proposals. At this point the two threads of narrative—of bloodthirsty Haman and beautiful Jewish queen–become intertwined. Mordecai, the guardian, persuades the reluctant Esther to intercede with the king. She has to decide whether to be the queen of a world-embracing empire or to identify with a threatened minority. Silence in a situation like this, a silence calculated to avoid endangering one's own life, can only lead to disaster (Esther 4:14). By interceding with the king, Esther risks her life.

Ahasuerus suddenly remembers that the Jew Mordecai had uncovered an earlier conspiracy; this rather artificial association illustrates one of the many weaknesses of this short novel that are in keeping with the mood but not the straight facts of history. The Jew-hater Haman is deprived of all his power and implores the Jewish queen to help him. Another touch of irony: his prostration is interpreted by Ahasuerus as attempted rape.

For the Jews, the danger of extermination by court intrigues has been averted, but that is not enough: there follows a scene of revenge in which 75,000 Persians from all provinces of the huge empire are massacred. Haman ends at the gallows he had erected for Mordecai, and at the specific request of the queen, his ten sons are also killed. This day is celebrated as the Purim Festival with music, dancing, masquerade, and stage plays. In the course of the narrative, Esther has become increasingly independent, and in the end she acts entirely on her own. But this independence cannot make us altogether happy, as it simply reinforces the old male patterns of retaliation and revenge as if there could be no real freedom and deliverance from the vicious circle of violence.

Above: Aert de Gelder (1645–1727) shows Mordecai talking intently to Esther, the daughter of his late uncle whom he has adopted. Mordecai has learned that Haman, a favorite of the king, intends to have all Jews killed.
National Museum, Budapest

Left: Through a messenger, Esther sends a letter to Mordecai advising him that the action he requires of her would be too dangerous. Miniature from MS 288, fol. 278, fifteenth century.
Chorherrenstift, Vorau

Under penalty of death it was forbidden to appear before the king without being asked. But Esther dares to implore the king to show mercy to the Jews. The king touches her with the tip of his scepter as a sign that she has nothing to fear. Panel from the Heilspiegel altar of Konrad Witz (1400–ca. 1444).
Kunstmuseum, Basel

Ancient and medieval sources

Joe H. Kirchberger

The book of Esther is set in the fifth century B.C. but was probably written down only during the second half of the second century B.C., as it seems to mirror the mood of the Jews at the time of the wars of the Maccabees. Apparently it is also meant to legitimate the origin of the Purim Festival, which was recognized officially only at a late date. This festival may have originated as a pagan celebration of spring, since it is observed during Adar, the sixth month of the Jewish calendar, around February-March. But it has also been assumed by some that the legend of Esther and Mordecai goes back to a Babylonian myth of Ishtar and Marduk, and that the Purim Festival is actually derived from the Babylonian New Year celebration. At any rate, the book seems to have been written by a Persian Jew.

ACCORDING TO JEWISH LEGEND, Solomon was the wisest and Ahasuerus the richest of all kings; the latter is described as an unstable, foolish ruler who in his wrath repudiates his favorites and then regrets his actions. He is said to have sent out for his great festival 3,333 messengers who spoke in seventy languages. His palace was so large that it could easily accommodate ten thousand guests with their servants and maids. No guest would drink twice from the same goblet, and the wine served was always one year older than the guest and had come from his home country. For every month of the six-month festival, the king displayed new treasures and sacred scrolls, as well as presents for his guests.

Queen Vashti was summoned before the king because of a debate among the guests. The Persians claimed that their women were the most beautiful, and the Medes said the same of their women. So Ahasuerus spoke: "My wife is neither Persian nor a Mede, yet she is the most beautiful one in my whole empire." And to prove it he ordered her brought before his guests.

Vashti was banished for her failure to cooperate. Jewish tradition even claims that Ahasuerus had her executed (and she would have deserved it, say some legends, because she had once prevented him from rebuilding the temple in Jerusalem). After Vashti's dismissal, beautiful virgins from all over the empire were summoned to his palace. Thousands arrived on camels or elephants, on horseback, or in state carriages. Each one was given seven maidservants. One day the king learned that a man in Susa (Sushan) named Mordecai had not brought his beautiful young niece to the palace. So he decreed a law that anyone hiding a beautiful virgin would be hanged. Mordecai was thus forced to take his niece to the palace.

Mordecai had come to Susa from Babylon where his parents had been taken as captives from Jerusalem. The original name of his niece was Hadassah, meaning "myrtle"; but when he kept her hidden in Susa he named her Esther, meaning "the concealed one," or ! "the one who conceals"—because for a long time she did not reveal her religion to her husband. When Esther came to the palace, she caused difficulties for Hegai, the chamberlain, because she asked for no jewelry and no clothes and did not touch any meat. The chamberlain was afraid the king would hold him, as supervisor of the harem, responsible and hang him. But Esther calmed him with her modest claim that "among so many virgins the king will not even notice me."

After a four-year preparation—so the legend has it—all girls were presented, and Esther stood among the richly decorated entirely unadorned in her natural grace. But the king descended from his throne, went straight toward her, and put the crown upon her head.

Esther was happy as a queen, but one thing troubled her: every day was a holiday and passed on like all the others, which made it difficult for her to remember the Sabbath, which she as a devout Jew wanted to observe. Then she thought of a way: to seven of her maids she gave new names that corresponded to the days of the week, and she ordered them to serve her always in the same order. Then she knew that when "Firmament" was waiting upon her, it was Sunday. "Workday" came on Monday, "Garden" on Tuesday, "Radiant" on Wednesday, "Quick" on Thursday, "Lamb" on Friday. And when "Rest" came to her, she knew it was the Sabbath. By this and other means she managed to preserve her piety in the palace of idolaters.

TRADITION EXPLAINS Haman's hatred of the Jews as follows: in his youth he had served in the army, and once he and his comrades had been cut off from the rest of the army. Haman had nothing left to eat or drink and was so desperate that he went to all his comrades asking for bread and water and vowing to serve his provider as a slave for the rest of his life. All his comrades rejected the offer as they needed their own supplies more than they desired a slave. Only one of the soldiers said: "If we will not be saved soon we shall starve anyway. Therefore come and share bread and water with me." Haman and his comrades were relieved the same day, and the incident was forgotten. He became rich, founded a family, and longed for power. So he moved to Susa and finally obtained the highest rank at the royal court. All had to bend before him, but one day he saw a man who did not. When he questioned him, the man answered: "I do not bend my head before one who vowed to be my slave." Now Haman recognized Mordecai and grew pale. He discussed this with his wife Seresh (or Zerish) who advised him to have Morde-cai killed so as to blot out the memory of his shameful vow. "That would be difficult," Haman replied, "for I have discovered that Mordecai is protected by the queen." "Then you must find a way to destroy not only Haman (Mordecai?) but all Jews in the one hundred and twenty kingdoms."

After that, Haman spent many sleepless nights and finally thought of a way to have all the Jews killed. He complained about them to the king, telling him they had too many holidays and hours for prayers and therefore worked too little, that they had caused Pharaoh's death in the Red Sea, that they had murdered his ancestor, Amalek, by tricks and deceit when Joshua had made the sun stand still, and that they had also killed Sisera, the great general, through the cunning of a woman (Jael).

When Mordecai heard of the edict against the Jews, he met three Jewish children coming home from school. When he asked them what they had learned that day, the first said: "Do not be afraid of sudden danger," and the second: "Let them talk, it will not get them anywhere," and the third: "I wish to bear the message and transmit to others." Mordecai took these sentences as a good omen, thanked the children, and told Haman when he met him: "I am enjoying the good news I received today out of the mouths of schoolchildren."

When Esther had arranged for the king to invite her and Haman for dinner, Seresh asked her husband: "Am I invited too?" "No," he replied, "only the queen and I." This infuriated Seresh. She had hated Vashti, who had never invited her, and she hated Esther, for she had hoped her own daughter would become queen. To calm her down, Haman remarked: "I met Mordecai this morning and am

In one of the corners of the Sistine Chapel, Michelangelo (1475–1564) depicts Esther's rescue of the Jews. At left: The king and Haman are Esther's guests. Center: Haman crucified. Right: Ahasuerus has the chronicle of the day brought to him.

glad I won't have to see him much longer." But Seresh sighed and said: "You cannot have him burned—remember how Abraham was saved in Nimrod's furnace. You cannot cut his throat—remember how Isaac was saved from Abraham's knife. You cannot drown him, as you know how Moses was pulled out of the Nile; you cannot throw him to the lions—think of Daniel; nor can you stone him—remember Goliath. Therefore, you must hang him!"

Esther is known as one of the seven prophetesses of the Jews, the others being Sarah, Miriam, Deborah, Hannah, Abigail, and Hulda.

JOSEPHUS TELLS ESTHER'S story in great detail and with several deviations from the biblical account. The Persian king is not Xerxes but his

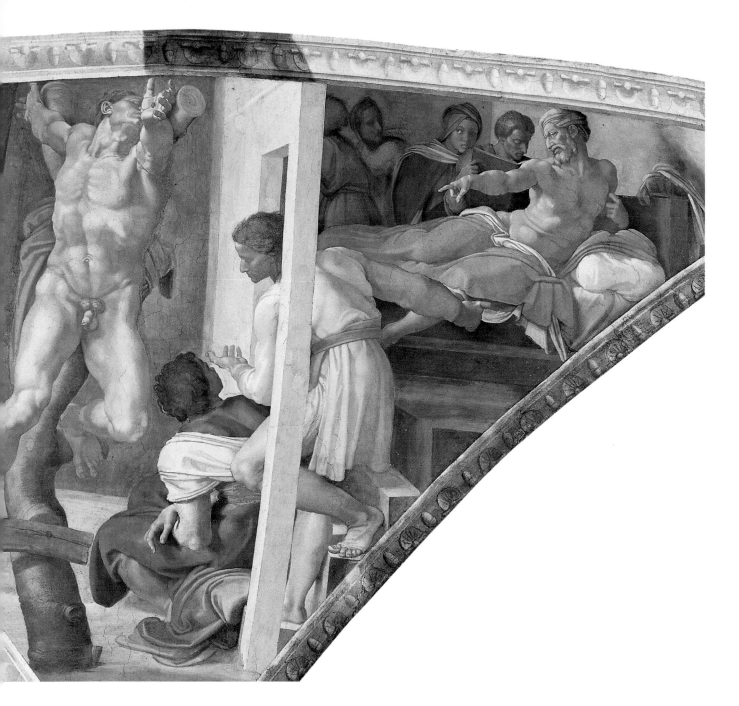

son Artaxerxes, and Haman is an enemy of the Jews mainly because he is an Amalekite, a member of a tribe the Jews had clashed with ever since their exodus from Egypt. After the king repudiates Vashti, Mordecai has no less than four hundred virgins prepared for the king, for six months. One of them is Esther. One of them is required to sleep with the king every night, but he rejects them all and sends them back—save Esther. When she finally stands before the king, he appears to her so awesome and fierce that she falls unconscious into the arms of her maids. Then, by a merciful act of God, the king's mood changes, and he embraces her and talks to her tenderly. When Haman sees himself threatened by death and begs Esther for mercy, he throws himself upon her bed. At this

moment the king enters and cries: "You most infamous of all men, do you want to do violence to my wife?" Now Haman is doomed. He is nailed to the same cross he had intended for Mordecai.

IN THE LATE Middle Ages there were numerous Purim plays, particularly among the Jewish population forced into the eastern part of Europe. Dante, too, knew Esther's story, though he mentions it only in passing. He says in the seventeenth canto of his *Purgatorio*: "Ahasuerus, the Great, stood by, / Esther, his wife, and worthy Mordecai; / Forever upright in his words and deeds."

The Woman with the Ointment

Matthew: chapter 26, verses 6–13
Luke: chapter 7, verses 36–50
John: chapter 12, verses 1–8

In many advanced cultures—in particular the Jewish culture—the anointing of the head became a legal act, particularly at the assumption of office by kings, priests, and high officials. The anointing was understood to transfer magical blessing and power to the anointed.

Now while Jesus was at Bethany in the house of Simon the leper, [7] a woman came to him with an alabaster jar of very costly ointment, and she poured it on his head as he sat at the table. [8] But when the disciples saw it, they were angry and said, "Why this waste? [9] For this ointment could have been sold for a large sum, and the money given to the poor." [10] But Jesus, aware of this, said to them, "Why do you trouble the woman? She has performed a good service for me. [11] For you always have the poor with you, but you will not always have me. [12] By pouring this ointment on my body she has prepared me for burial. [13] Truly I tell you, wherever this good news is proclaimed in the whole world, what she has done will be told in remembrance of her."

7 [36] One of the Pharisees asked Jesus to eat with him, and he went into the Pharisee's house and took his place at the table. [37] And a woman in the

city, who was a sinner, having learned that he was eating in the Pharisee's house, brought an alabaster jar of ointment. [38] She stood behind him at his feet, weeping, and began to bathe his feet with her tears and to dry them with her hair. Then she continued kissing his feet and anointing them with the ointment. [39] Now when the Pharisee who had invited him saw it, he said to himself, "If this man were a prophet, he would have known who and what kind of woman this is who is touching him—that she is a sinner." [40] Jesus spoke up and said to him, "Simon, I have something to say to you." "Teacher," he replied, "Speak." [41] "A certain creditor had two debtors; one owed five hundred denarii, and the other fifty. [42] When they could not pay, he canceled the debts for both of them. Now which of them will love him more?" [43] Simon answered, "I suppose the one for whom he canceled the greater debt." And Jesus said to him, "You have judged rightly." [44] Then turning toward the woman, he said to Simon, "Do you see this woman? I entered your house; you gave me no water for my feet, but she has bathed my feet with her tears and dried them with her hair. [45] You gave me no kiss, but from the time I came in she has not stopped kissing my feet. [46] You did not anoint my head with oil, but she has anointed my feet with ointment. [47] Therefore, I tell you, her sins, which were many, have been forgiven; hence she has shown great love. But the one to whom little is forgiven, loves little." [48] Then he said to her, "Your sins are forgiven." [49] But those who were at the table with him began to say among themselves, "Who is this who even forgives sins?" [50] And he said to the woman, "Your faith has saved you; go in peace."

12 Six days before the Passover Jesus came to Bethany, the home of Lazarus, whom he had raised from the dead. [2] There they gave a dinner for him. Martha served, and Lazarus was one of those at the table with him. [3] Mary took a pound of costly perfume made of pure nard, anointed Jesus' feet, and wiped them with her hair. The house was filled with the fragrance of the perfume. [4] But Judas Iscariot, one of his disciples (the one who was about to betray him), said, [5] "Why was this perfume not sold for three hundred denarii and the money given to the poor?" [6] (He said this not because he cared about the poor, but because he was a thief; he kept the common purse and used to steal what was put into it.) [7] Jesus said, "Leave her alone. She bought it so that she might keep it for the day of my burial. [8] You always have the poor with you, but you do not always have me."

Pages 118/119: During a supper at the home of Simon, Mary Magdalene anoints Jesus' feet. Fresco in the basilica at San Angelo in Formis, eleventh century.

Left: The upper part of the central panel of the triptych by Lukas Moser, the so-called Magdalene altar *at the parish church in Tiefenbronn (ca. 1431), shows Mary Magdalene washing Jesus' feet with her tears.*

The Woman with the Ointment: nameless but not forgotten

Dorothee Soelle

The story of the woman who, shortly before Jesus' death, anointed him with precious oil contains a paradox which in some way is typical of the role of women in Western religious tradition. Jesus, deeply touched by what the woman has done, utters these great, thoughtful words: "Truly I tell you, wherever this good news is proclaimed in the whole world, what she has done will be told in remembrance of her" (Matt. 26:13). But this very woman whose memory stands in the center of the gospel has not even a traditional name. How, then, can one remember her? Not even Jesus' solemn bidding has prevented her from remaining nameless. She fades from view behind so many men's names, like so much else that Jesus intended to highlight but that, historically, became obscured by other priorities of the men's world.

The widely divergent versions of the anointing story as told by the four evangelists already display this tendency. Luke's assumption is that the woman is a prostitute, and his emphasis is that her sins are being forgiven. The earlier version I am following here does not warrant such a conclusion. But all the variations hint at something disreputable, scandalous in the story; at any rate, an infraction of tradition, custom, and taboo is taking place.

In this miniature from the Codex Egberti, *fol. 65v, Mary, sister of Martha and Lazarus, anoints Jesus' feet.*
Stadtbibliothek, Trier

The place is Simon's house in Bethany, a village separated from Jerusalem by only a valley. A woman enters and goes to the table where Jesus is invited for supper. In general women were excluded from such events; at best they might appear as hostesses. But this woman walks right into the group of men. In the house of a leper even touching is taboo, but with her gesture she establishes a physical intimacy with the one who will soon be led away to his death. She does not say a word, but acts. Without speaking she violates several taboos, as if she had, in our day, entered one of those exclusive men's clubs, or, ignoring all cautionary measures, had approached an AIDS patient. And this after centuries of warnings about women's preoccupation with extravagant finery and pleasure-seeking!

She breaks an alabaster flask and pours the oil on Jesus' head. It is a luxury oil that belongs in the homes of the rich and the palaces of kings, not in the house of a simple Jewish man. The value of this precious article is estimated at three hundred denarii, equivalent to the annual wages of a farm-hand (if he was lucky enough to find work for three hundred days in a year). But she does not care, she gives away all she has. She also suffers the indignation of the other invited guests who snap at her and try to chase her away. She pays no attention, completely absorbed in what she is doing.

Exegetes have offered various explanations for the woman's conduct, which is extravagant indeed. Many have focused exclusively on the contrast between assistance for the poor and luxury for Jesus, and have forgotten what the woman actually did. Some, like the disciples, give the impression of having to conceal their discomfort with this woman's story. Others have seen in the pouring of the oil upon the head of Jesus a reference to the prophets' anointing of Israel's kings. But Jesus is close to his execution, and soon nobody will believe him to be the "King of the Jews." Still the woman treats him like a king. She decorates the body of one who will soon be tortured to death as the most contemptible of men. Does she render him this service because she has a premonition of what is about to happen? Perhaps she knows better than the male disciples who do not wish to hear about suffering and death.

There is an old objection to Christianity, from antiquity through Nietzsche to our own day, which claims it to be anti-body, ascetic, stingy, and unsensual. A Roman writer, Minucius Felix, criticizes the Christian life and mocks the Christians as *pallidi trepidi,* "trembling palefaces." "You do not decorate your heads with flowers," he charged. "You begrudge your body fragrant scents. You save your ointments for the corpses, but refuse your graves wreaths of flowers, you trembling palefaces. . . . Thus, you poor people will live neither after death nor before death."

The nameless woman from Bethany is a wonderful refutation of this deep-seated suspicion. She represents the hidden part of the story. She has celebrated Jesus' life in the face of his death; without words she has expressed her love for him and at the same time established a symbol for the high value of life, as sensuously, cheerfully, and extravagantly as imaginable.

The mystics had a beautiful expression for such useless, self-forgetful action in which being and doing become one and where one ceases to be concerned about appearances. They called it the state of sunder Warumbe, of "without the why." In this happy, oblivious condition, one is no longer preoccupied with questions that render our lives trivial. The woman of Bethany did not ask what it cost, what it would bring, what effect it would have, or if it would do her any harm. She must have crossed the border of caution, prudence, and concern for self-esteem, of calculating the whole life for the sake of a purpose-oriented rationalism. Like the poor widow (Mark 12:42; Luke 21:2), she gave everything, she gave herself—a gratuitous gift of a nameless but unforgotten woman.

On the panel of an altar by Nicolas Froment (ca. 1430–1483/86?) painted in 1461, a woman anoints Jesus' feet with precious oil at a feast in Bethany.
Galleria degli Uffizi, Florence

Ancient and medieval sources

Joe H. Kirchberger

In recounting one of the most beautiful and famous scenes of the New Testament, the evangelists differ quite widely. Matthew and Mark agree almost word for word with Matthew's version, obviously depending on the earlier narrative of Mark. In both of those Gospels the scene takes place at the house of Simon the Leper and the woman entering pours the precious oil on Jesus' head. In Luke the event is said to take place in the house of a Pharisee, but since Jesus later addresses him as "Simon," he is doubtless the same person

A woman anoints Jesus' feet. When Judas grumbles that the woman should have sold the precious oil to distribute the money among the poor, Jesus says: "For you always have the poor with you; but you will not always have me. By pouring this ointment on my body she has prepared me for burial." MS 139/1363, fol. 15v from the Miroir de l'Humaine Salvation, fifteenth century. Musée Condé, Chantilly

mentioned by the other two texts. Luke refers to the woman as a sinner, a designation missing in the other Gospels. John locates the scene in the house of the sisters Mary and Martha, and Mary is the one anointing Jesus. Both Luke and John record the woman anointing Jesus' feet, not his head.

The anointed one is in Israel the royal deputy of the Lord God. The word *messiah*, derived from the Hebrew hammaschiacha and the Aramaic meschiacha means "anointed one." Anointing became a custom in the Western world too: since 751, when Pippin the Short, father of Charlemagne, ascended the throne, German kings have been anointed; and Byzantine emperors were anointed as early as 1000. The anointed one thus became the Christus Domini, the "Anointed of the Lord," for the Greek word *christos* also means "anointed."

In all these ceremonies the head was anointed. Washing the feet, on the other hand, was a particular act of hospitality. Thus Luke reproaches Jesus' host for not giving him water for his feet. In Matthew's and Mark's versions, it is quite possible that the woman wanted, consciously or subconsciously, to crown Jesus by anointing him, making him king of the Jews. But Jesus himself interpreted the anointment as preparation for his forthcoming entombment.

SOME COMMENTATORS have questioned some of the details of Luke's version, arguing that no Pharisee would have admitted a "sinner," apparently a whore, into his house. The Pharisees were a particularly strict religious party that stressed meticulous observance of Moses' laws. Other interpreters have assumed that the Pharisee may have invited the sinner in order to test Jesus' prophetic gifts.

Jesus' famous statement: "For you will always have the poor with you; but you will not always have me" has given rise to countless debates. Some have seen in it a certain indifference on the part of Jesus to the plight of the poor, a view of poverty as a necessary evil that cannot be remedied. But this, of course, is contradicted by many of his other words and deeds. Here Jesus seems to have been acutely conscious of his approaching death, and the main import of his words was to draw to his disciples' attention the shortness of the time remaining.

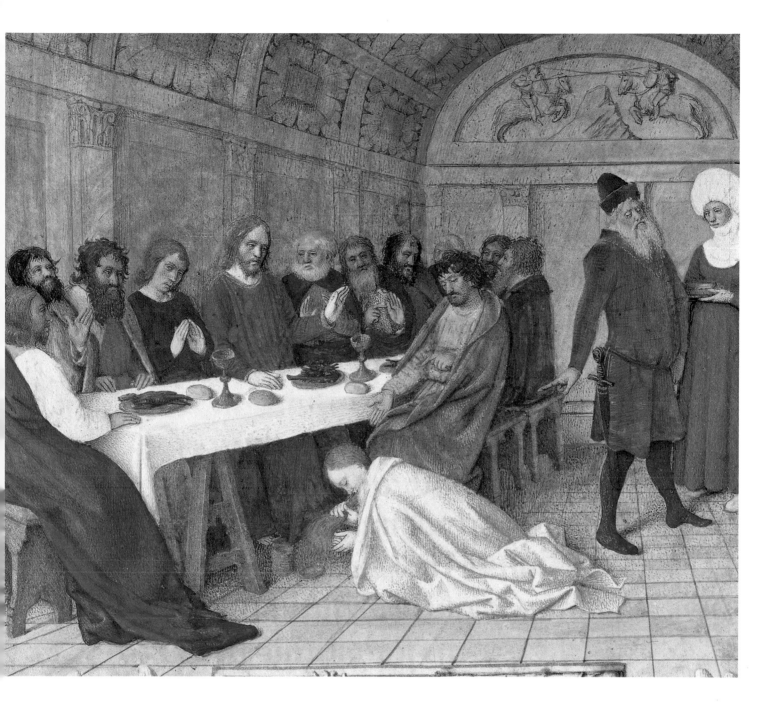

The women discussed in this and the next two chapters, all of whom have close contact with Jesus, are clearly separate characters, at least in the first three Gospels. But already with the Gospel of John (12:1–8) the "anointing woman" is equated with Mary of Bethany, sister of Martha and Lazarus. In the legends of the early Middle Ages, starting with Gregory the Great (around 600), the characters of Mary Magdalene, Mary of Bethany, and the woman with the ointment, who has no name in the Synoptic Gospels, are merged. Some of the confusion arises from the number of women in Jesus' circle who were named Mary—from his own mother to Mary of Bethany, Mary Magdalene, and Mary the mother of James (the "Less"). Also contributing to the legends is Mary of Egypt, not mentioned in the Bible but probably historical who, after a life of sin in Alexandria, spent forty-seven years in penitence in the Syrian Desert, east of the Jordan River.

At the house of Simon, a woman bathes Jesus' feet with her tears, dries them with her hair, and then pours consecrated oil over them. Detail from a miniature by Jean Fouquet (1420–1481), from the Book of Hours of Etienne Chevalier, *MS fr. 71, fol. 37.*
Musée Condé, Chantilly

Mary and Martha

Luke: chapter 10, verses 38–42
John: chapter 11, verses 1–45

With Mary and Martha we meet, after Lot's daughters and Rachel and Leah, the Bible's third pair of sisters. Similar to Rachel and Leah, Mary and Martha are entirely different in character. Martha is the extrovert, the busy one, Mary the introvert, concerned only with the salvation of her soul.

Opposite: Mary is so engrossed in her conversation with Jesus that she is unaware of her sister Martha asking for her help in preparing the dinner. Painting by Tintoretto (1518–1594). Alte Pinakothek, Munich

Pages 126/127: Jesus with Martha and Mary. Flemish painting in the church Saint-Gervais, Paris

Now as they went on their way, he entered a certain village, where a woman named Martha welcomed him into her home. 39 She had a sister named Mary, who sat at the Lord's feet and listened to what he was saying. 40 But Martha was distracted by her many tasks; so she came to him and asked, "Lord, do you not care that my sister has left me to do all the work by myself? Tell her then to help me." 41 But the Lord answered her, "Martha, Martha, you are worried and distracted by many things; 42 there is need of only one thing. Mary has chosen the better part, which will not be taken away from her."

11 Now a certain man was ill, Lazarus of Bethany, the village of Mary and her sister Martha. 2 Mary was the one who anointed the Lord with perfume and wiped his feet with her hair; her brother Lazarus was ill. 3 So the sisters sent a message to Jesus, "Lord, he whom you love is ill." 4 But when Jesus heard it, he said, "This illness does not lead to death; rather it is for God's glory, so that the Son of God may be glorified through it. 5 Accordingly, though Jesus loved Martha and her sister and Lazarus, 6 after having heard that Lazarus was ill, he stayed two days longer in the place where he was.

7 Then after this he said to the disciples, "Let us go to Judea again." 8 The disciples said to him, "Rabbi, the Jews were just now trying to stone you, and are you going there again?" 9 Jesus answered, "Are there not twelve hours of daylight? Those who walk during the day do not stumble, because they see the light of this world. 10 But those who walk at night stumble, because the light is not in them." 11 After saying this, he told them, "Our friend Lazarus has fallen asleep, but I am going there to awaken him." 12 The disciples said to him, "Lord, if he has fallen asleep, he will be all right." 13 Jesus, however, had been speaking about his death, but they thought that he was referring merely to sleep. 14 Then Jesus told them plainly, "Lazarus is dead. 15 For your sake I am glad I was not there, so that you may believe. But let us go to him." 16 Thomas, who was called the Twin, said to his fellow disciples, "Let us also go, that we may die with him."

17 When Jesus arrived, he found that Lazarus had already been in the tomb four days. 18 Now Bethany was near Jerusalem, some two miles away, 19 and many of the Jews had come to Martha and Mary to console them about their brother. 20 When Martha heard that Jesus was coming, she went and met him, while Mary stayed at home. 21 Martha said to Jesus, "LORD, if you had been here, my brother would not have died. 22 But even now I

IACOBVS TINTORET••• F.

know that God will give you whatever you ask of him." ²³ Jesus said to her, "Your brother will rise again." ²⁴ Martha said to him, "I know that he will rise again in the resurrection on the last day." ²⁵ Jesus said to her, "I am the resurrection and the life. Those who believe in me, even though they die, will live, ²⁶ and everyone who lives and believes in me will never die. Do you believe this?" ²⁷ She said to him, "Yes, Lord, I believe that you are the Messiah, the Son of God, the one coming into the world."

²⁸ When she had said this, she went back and called her sister Mary, and told her privately, "The Teacher is here and is calling for you." ²⁹ And when she heard it, she got up quickly and went to him. ³⁰ Now Jesus had not yet come to the village, but was still at the place where Martha had met him. ³¹ The Jews who were with her in the house, consoling her, saw Mary get up quickly and go out. They followed her because they thought that she was going to the tomb to weep there. ³² When Mary came where Jesus was and saw him, she knelt at his feet and said to him, "LORD, if you had been here, my brother would not have died." ³³ When Jesus saw her weeping, and the Jews who came with her also weeping, he was greatly disturbed in spirit and deeply moved. ³⁴ He said, "Where have you laid him?" They said to him, "Lord, come and see." ³⁵ Jesus began to weep. ³⁶ So the Jews said, "See how he loved him!" ³⁷ But some of them said, "Could not he who opened the eyes of the blind man have kept this man from dying?"

³⁸ Then Jesus, again greatly disturbed, came to the tomb. It was a cave, and a stone was lying against it. ³⁹ Jesus said, "Take away the stone." Martha, the sister of the dead man, said to him, "LORD, already there is a stench because he has been dead four days." ⁴⁰ Jesus said to her, "Did I not tell you that if you believed, you would see the glory of God?" ⁴¹ So they took away the stone. And Jesus looked upward and said, "Father, I thank you for having heard me. ⁴² I knew that you always hear me, but I have said this for the sake of the crowd standing here, so that they may believe that you sent me." ⁴³ When he had said this, he cried with a loud voice, "Lazarus, come out!" ⁴⁴ The dead man came out, his hands and feet bound with strips of cloth, and his face wrapped in a cloth. Jesus said to them, "Unbind him, and let him go."

⁴⁵ Many of the Jews therefore, who had come with Mary and had seen what Jesus did, believed in him.

When Mary came
where Jesus was and saw him,
she knelt at his feet and said to him,
"Lord, if you had been here, my
brother would not have died."
John 11:32

*In the left panel of a Lazarus
triptych by Nicolas Froment
(ca. 1435–1484) Martha kneels
before Jesus, saying: "If you had
been here, my brother would
not have died."
Galleria degli Uffizi, Florence*

Unity of acting and dreaming

Dorothee Soelle

Rereading the story of Mary and Martha, I was reminded of my childhood. In our Protestant church in a suburb of Cologne there was a glass window with the inscription: Eins ist not! (One thing is needed). Mary, lost to the world shyly and fragile, is sitting at Jesus' feet. Martha stands nearby, leaning against the table, legs apart and holding a mixing bowl. She raises one hand in reproach: "Lord, do you not care that my sister has left me to do all the work by myself?" (Luke 10:40). I remember that I did not like the story.

Western tradition has seen these two women as types or figures of the contemplative and the active, as meditativeness and industry, relaxed listening and restless caring for the body's daily requirements. They were not only juxtaposed but ranked according to an order of values formulated rather by Aristotle than by Jewish thought. Contemplative life is judged to be superior, more spiritual and essential, while active, practical life is treated as necessary but inferior. Mary has "chosen the better part" (Luke 10:42) while Martha in this tradition is seen as useful but somewhat narrow and limited. Western thinking has been predisposed to regard "pure" theory above mere practice, as intellectual labor above manual labor. The Reformation pushed aside the meditations of contemplative monks and nuns in favor of practical work, yet Martha's image as that of the active and pragmatic woman was even further degraded. Luther said: "Martha, your work must be punished and regarded for nothing. . . . I do not want any work but Mary's, and that is faith."

This spiritualizing and anti-Jewish tradition of interpretation in favor of Mary and against Martha was counteracted not by the Reformation but by an entirely different movement: that of the mystics. Meister Eckhart (ca. 1260–1328), in a radically novel interpretation (Sermon 28) moved the still immature Mary to the initial stage of spiritual life but regarded the mature and experienced Martha as having closer proximity to what is needed. "Martha was afraid that her sister would get stuck in sweetness and well-being" he observes. Martha wishes Mary to be like herself. And Eckhart continues his inspired Christian but nonclerical reinterpretation, one which reflects the spirit of the flourishing women's movement in the late Middle Ages:

"Therefore Christ said and meant: Be calm, Martha, she, too, has chosen the good part. This part will get lost from her but the highest good will be bestowed upon her: She will be blessed like you."[1]

Today's women consciously engaging in Christian tradition are beginning to learn to differentiate between the antifeminine and the liberating features of this tradition. For our story this means taking steps: first, rediscover Martha, and second, get Mary and Martha together! We must not just "understand" Martha, but we must revise our estimation of her, realize her strength, and make her power our own; we must see her not only as she is portrayed in Luke 10, but also as she appears in John 11, the story of Lazarus's raising from the dead, in which Martha is the active one who argues with Jesus as Job did with God. She acts pragmatically, knowing that after four days in the grave her brother will stink, and she thinks theologically when she confesses to Christ: "Yes, Lord: I believe that you are the Messiah, the Son of God, the one coming into the world" (John 11:27), as only Peter among the disciples does. To rediscover this Christian woman[2] will help us to take the power away from hierarchy, even if it has crept into ourselves—hierarchy as guaranteed domination that does not have to justify itself, which imparts privileges and superiority and is always directed against the most profound interests of women even when it appears among women, as in the case of Mary and Martha. Hierarchical thinking always supports the contempt, ridiculing, and trivialization of women, and I believe that this is what I felt as a little girl. I felt sorry for Martha; she embarrassed me. It pained and disturbed me that women could be like that Martha cliché I had inherited.

It helps me to rediscover Martha, the strong, self-assured, down-to-earth, lucid woman. In the story of Lazarus, we are also told how differently the two sisters reacted to their brother's death. Mary throws herself at Jesus' feet, crying: Martha argues that he had been close by and could easily have come. She is impertinent, she does not give in, and it is she who tells the truth, a female Peter. It is no accident that in later times she was presented as a dragon killer.

Connected with the rediscovery of vilified Martha is the other necessary step of interpretation, extremely important for today's women and men: we do not have to choose between contemplation and action. No one has the right to impose such a choice upon us. We do not have to divide the world between doers and dreamers, between Mary, gentle, attentive, and devoted on the one hand, and Martha, practical and energetic on the other. We need both. In fact, we are both these sisters. Teresa of Avila, who follows the interpretation of the mystics and rejects self-isolating contemplation, says: "Believe me, Martha and Mary must be together to accommodate the Lord and keep him with them forever; otherwise he will be served poorly and remain hungry. How could Mary who always sat at his feet have offered him food if her sister had not jumped in? And his food is our gathering souls, that they may be saved and praise him in eternity."[3] Only both sisters together can "accommodate" Christ to give him a place in the world.

In our affluent world there exists a great longing for spirituality, absorption, contemplation, and mysticism. Mary may become the symbol of this incomplete, immature spirituality. Many young people despair of the chance to take action in our world; they see the trees dying, the children of the poor starving, and they retreat into the introspection the mystics have warned against. Eckhart says of Mary that when she sat at Christ's feet "her name was not yet Mary. For she was still sitting feeling well and full of sweet sentiments, she had been taken to school and was learning to live. But Martha stood there, substantially present."

I have to think of this differentiation when I look at the strong women of my generation who act staunchly, fighting the dragons dominating us. Clearly and unequivocally they have broken with the racists in South Africa, they have stood in front of supermarkets and talked to people in the little corner shop, they have visited bank managers and said clearly and audibly what they think. In the groups of women who for years have organized the boycott against the "fruits of apartheid," I see many Marthas together, and also among those women who have surrounded the dragon who lives in the Pentagon, and begun to resist. This is the Martha Meister Eckhart saw, whom the people of southern France have presented as a killer of dragons, and who, according to another folktale, crossed the ocean with her sister Mary to teach and preach. If one day our churches will "accommodate" Christ and offer him food, then such women will be bishops and teachers of the church. The Martha in me will not supersede Mary. Within each woman there should still be the young girl she once was. But the best women I know will no longer accept the separation of the two.

Clearly Mary and Martha of the Bible also represent a mother-daughter problem. But the Bible turns mothers and daughters into sisters, and legend lets both cross the ocean with Jesus' disciples to teach and preach, making them act and dream, do the good work and pray, uniting struggle and reflection and, in the process, making the world itself more sisterly.

Opposite: Raising of Lazarus, *painting by Rembrandt van Rijn (1606–1669). County Museum of Art, Los Angeles*

Pages 132/133: Pieter Aertsen (1508–1575) painted a number of genre pictures that include a small biblical scene in the background. In this painting the foreground depicts preparations for a sumptuous meal in the house of Lazarus, while in the background a small group is listening to Jesus' words. Museum Boymans-van Beuningen, Rotterdam

Notes

1. Meister Eckhart, *Deutsche Predigten und Traktate* (Munich, 1969), 286.
2. E. Moltmann-Wendel, *Ein eigener Mensch werden, Trauer um Jesus* (Gütersloh, 1980).
3. J. Sudbrack, *Erfahrungen einer Liebe, Teresa d'Avilas Mystik als Begegnung mit Gott* (Freiburg, 1979).

Ancient and medieval sources

Joe H. Kirchberger

The name Martha comes from the Aramaic, the Semitic *lingua franca* in the Near East at the time of Christ, and means "mistress." But the name Mary (Maria), or Miriam in Hebrew, which appears time and again in the New Testament and has remained one of the most popular of all female first names, cannot be explained definitively. According to the Jewish-Hellenistic philosopher Philo of Alexandria, it means "hope," according to others "recalcitrance," from *mara*—"to resist"

Above: In the Book of Hours *of Catherine of Cleve, from the first half of the fifteenth century, Martha is depicted with spoon and kettle, characterizing her as an efficient housewife. Miniature in the petitionary prayer section.*
Pierpont Morgan Library, New York

Opposite: Mary listens to the words of Jesus. Two of his disciples are standing behind him. Martha enters the room and amiably turns her head toward Jesus, asking him to admonish Mary because she is not helping her prepare the meal. The gowns of the two women and the furnishing of the room indicate that Lazarus and his sisters are quite well-to-do. Painting by Jacob Jordaens (1593–1678). Musée des Beaux-Arts, Lille

(or possibly "bitterness"); and some have suggested "well proportioned"—beautiful. Someone has even proposed a derivation from the Egyptian *mr* (love) + *jam* (= Jahwe?).

The story of Lazarus being raised from the dead and of his sisters Mary and Martha was well known to all fathers of the church during the first Christian centuries. Particularly important was the so-called *Diatessaron,* a "harmony" of the four Gospels by Tatian, which Abbot Hrabanus Maurus translated from the Latin into Old High German as early as A.D. 830. Tatian was a Syrian apologist of the second century, a defender of the Christian faith against all attacks from the then prevailing Hellenistic philosophy, and one of the founders of scientific Christian theology. The Old Saxonian Heliand of around the same time, which describes the life of Jesus according to the Gospels but makes him a sort of popular king, also mentions Lazarus and his sisters, and so does the slightly later Evangeliar of Otfried von Weissenburg of Alsace. These early medieval works neither elaborate nor alter the description of Mary and Martha given in the Gospels. Yet the incompletely preserved *Rheinauer Paulus,* written in the beginning of the twelfth century at the Rheinau monastery near Schaffhausen, and the contemporary so-called St. Trudperter Song of Songs already develop their characters further: they appear once as imploring sisters and once as symbols of spiritual (Mary) and worldly (Martha) life.

ENTIRELY NEW FEATURES are added in the Legenda Aurea of Jacobus a Voragine, archbishop of Genoa, the most important medieval collection of legends, written down around 1270. According to him, Martha belongs to a Syrian royal family. In particular he tells the story of the sisters after Christ's resurrection when his followers were suffering from persecutions by the Jews. Then three holy men and three holy women were put in a boat without sails, helm, or rudder: Mary and Martha, Marcilla, their maid, with Lazarus, Maximinus—who had baptized the siblings—and Cedon, a blind man who had been cured by Jesus. All were taken miraculously across the sea and landed in France at a spot which is now Marseilles. There they fled into the vestibule of a pagan temple. Later Lazarus became the first bishop of Marseilles while Martha founded

a convent of pious virgins; she is said to have lived for another thirty years of severe penance and contemplation.

ACCORDING TO LEGENDS of the fourteenth century, Martha also converted sinful Mary Magdalene to Christianity, and this motif has entered into several German and Dutch passion plays. In other late medieval legends, Martha is said to be Simon's wife. She is also supposed to have subdued a dragon at Tarascon in southern France. Finally, some stories are told about miracles surrounding her death: when she lay dying and her attendants were asleep, a gust of wind blew out the candles and Martha saw a swarm of evil spirits entering. She stammered: "My father Eli (Lord), my dear guest, my seducers want to devour me; they have written down the evil I did. Eli, stay with me and help!" Then she saw her sister come in and relight the candles, and Christ came in and summoned her.

On the same day, Bishop Fronto in Périgueux (Dordogne) fell asleep on his pulpit during the service. Then God appeared to him and said: "If you wish to keep your promise to Martha, our hostess, follow me!" Immediately they were in Tarascon and took Martha to her grave. She still performed miracles from her grave: thus Chlodwig, king of the Franks who had converted to Christianity, was cured by her of a kidney ailment. Martha is also said to have put a picture of Jesus in her garden, and all plants touching it had healing power. Emperor Julian Apostata (called the "Renegade" because he had reverted to paganism) had the picture removed and replaced by others, but they had no miraculous powers.

Mary of Magdala

John
Chapter 19, verses 25–27; Chapter 20, verses 1–18
Matthew
Chapter 27, verses 54–56
Mark
Chapter 16, verses 9–11
Luke
Chapter 24, verses 10–11

Mary of Magdala, usually called Mary Magdalene, is, after the Virgin Mary, probably the best-known woman figure of the New Testament, and as such has been treated time and time again in words and pictures.

Meanwhile, standing near the cross of Jesus were his mother, and his mother's sister, Mary the wife of Clopas, and Mary Magdalene. 26 When Jesus saw his mother and the disciple whom he loved standing beside her, he said to his mother, "Woman, here is your son." 27 Then he said to the disciple, "Here is your mother." And from that hour the disciple took her into his own home.

20 Early on the first day of the week, while it was still dark, Mary Magdalene came to the tomb and saw that the stone had been removed from the tomb. 2 So she ran and went to Simon Peter and the other disciple, the one whom Jesus loved, and said to them, "They have taken the Lord out of the tomb, and we do not know where they have laid him." 3 Then Peter and the other disciple set out and went toward the tomb. 4 The two were running together, but the other disciple outran Peter and reached the tomb first. 5 He bent down to look in and saw the linen wrappings lying there, but he did not go in. 6 Then Simon Peter came, following him, and went into the tomb. He saw the linen wrappings lying there, 7 and the cloth that had been on Jesus' head, not lying with the linen wrappings but rolled up in a place by itself. 8 Then the other disciple, who reached the tomb first, also went in, and he saw and believed; 9 for as yet they did not understand the scripture, that he must rise from the dead. 10 Then the disciples returned to their homes.
11 But Mary stood weeping outside the tomb. As she wept, she bent over to look into the tomb; 12 and she saw two angels in white, sitting where the body of Jesus had been lying, one at the head and the other at the feet. 13 They said to her, "Woman, why are you weeping?" She said to them, "They have taken away my Lord, and I do not know where they have laid him." 14 When she had said this, she turned around and saw Jesus standing there, but she did not know that it was Jesus. 15 Jesus said to her, "Woman, why are you weeping? Whom are you looking for?" Supposing him to be the gardener, she said to him, "Sir, if you have carried him away, tell me where you have laid him, and I will take him away." 16 Jesus said to her, "Mary!" She turned and said to him in Hebrew, "Rabbouni!" (which means Teacher). 17 Jesus said to her, "Do not hold on to me, because I have not yet ascended to the Father. But go to my brothers and say to them, 'I am ascending to my Father and your Father, to my God and your God.'" 18 Mary Magdalene went and announced to the disciples, "I have seen the Lord"; and she told them that he had said these things to her.

27 [54] Now when the centurion and those with him, who were keeping watch over Jesus, saw the earthquake and what took place, they were terrified and said, "Truly this man was God's Son!" [55] Many women were also there, looking on from a distance; they had followed Jesus from Galilee and had provided for him. [56] Among them were Mary Magdalene, and Mary the mother of James and Joseph, and the mother of the sons of Zebedee.

16 [9] Now after he rose early on the first day of the week, he appeared first to Mary Magdalene, from whom he had cast out seven demons. [10] She went out and told those who had been with him, while they were mourning and weeping. [11] But when they heard that he was alive and had been seen by her, they would not believe it.

24 [10] Now it was Mary Magdalene, Joanna, Mary the mother of James, and the other women with them who told this to the apostles. [11] But these words seemed to them an idle tale, and they did not believe them.

Page 136: Mary Magdalene with an ointment vessel in her hand. Miniature from the petitionary prayer section of Catherine of Cleve's Book of Hours (fifteenth century).
Pierpont Morgan Library, New York

Page 137: Mary Magdalene has retreated as a penitent into a cavern where she prays perpetually and remorsefully. José de Ribera, called Lo Spagno-letto (1591–1652), has given an ointment vessel to the saint as an attribute which stands at the lower left on a step of rocks.
Museo del Prado, Madrid

Right: William Etty (1787–1849), main exponent of English Romantic painting, presents on a large horizontal canvas the Easter morning scene in which Mary Magdalene encounters two angels at the open grave whose guard has fallen asleep, and then sees the risen Christ himself suddenly standing before her.
Tate Gallery, London

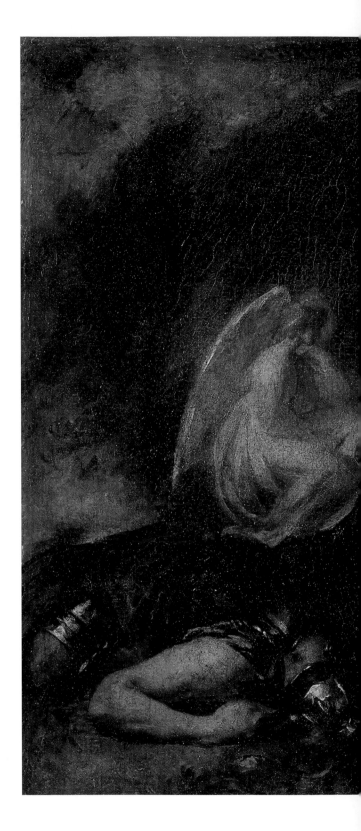

*Above: Lucas Cranach the Elder (1472–1553)
presents Mary Magdalene as a rich, courtly
woman, covered with precious jewelry, who
is fully aware of her beauty.
Wallraf-Richartz-Museum, Cologne*

*Right: Jan von Scorel (1495–1562) represents
Mary Magdalene sitting under a tree in a relaxed
posture against a fantastic mountain landscape, a
beautiful woman posing as a model for a painter.
With deliberate elegance she rests her left hand
on the folds of her gown.
Rijksmuseum Stichting, Amsterdam*

"Woman, why are you weeping?"

Dorothee Soelle

Mary Magdalene, "apostle of the apostles," as Augustine called her, is one of the most prominent female figures of Christian tradition. She has played a leading role in the original Jesus movement as well as in the later tradition of the church in cultural history. But these two roles do not agree with each other. Historically Mary from Magdala at the Lake of Gennesaret is one of the well-to-do women who has followed the itinerant rabbi Jesus throughout Galilee after she had been "healed of evil spirits and infirmities" (Luke 8:2). She goes with him to Jerusalem, witnesses the crucifixion at Golgotha, and is the first person to whom the resurrected Christ shows himself.

In later centuries we have an entirely different picture in which two New Testament traditions are combined. A church increasingly dominated by men needed the image of a "great sinner," attractive for her very remorse and penitence, in order to legitimate its own sexual repression and antifeminism. Mary Magdalene became the symbol of the "fallen girl." Sin was, in clear contrast to the Bible, exclusively related to sexual conduct. Why, women ask today, is there no "great male sinner" in this tradition? And how would it look if, for instance, one would have turned Peter into a converted procurer?

Peter and Mary Magdalene have been the leading personalities of the Jesus movement. Both worked in the early communities, attested their faith, lived for love, preached the gospel, and did missionary work. Quite early. as mentioned in the later apocryphal gospels, there were conflicts between men and women. "Would the Redeemer have spoken secretly to a woman without letting us know? Are we all to turn around and listen to her?" an angry, jealous Peter complains in the apocryphal Gospel according to Mary Magdalena. This male fear of women usurping power undermined the originally just, egalitarian community of equals.

The Gospels preserve a record of Jesus' special relationship with women, possibly most distinctly with respect to the person who in her lifetime was closest to Jesus, Mary of Magdala. Her healing from her illness meant, as a matter of course, also her being called unto the path Jesus had gone.

She follows, "serves" him; this is an expression for her devoting her life, and maybe makes a little more comprehensible her identification with the great sinner in Luke 7. Before Mary Magdalene met Jesus, she was possessed by seven demons (Luke 8:2), which would indicate mental illness, possibly a manic-depressive or epileptic condition. Then the formerly insane woman moves with other women to Jerusalem, beholds the cross "afar off" when all the disciples have forsaken Jesus and fled (Matthew 26:56 KJV). She goes to the grave and is the first to see Christ resurrected (John 20:1, 14).

What she and the other women have done becomes clear only if one understands the policy of the Roman Empire against those regarded as rebels. The crucifixion of a person had dire consequences for all relatives and friends. Criminal justice ordered that a crucified criminal, as a warning example, should hang on the cross until animals had eaten his corpse. Refusal of a funeral was normative and meant to punish relatives, friends, and, as in Jesus' case, followers as well. Therefore crucified bodies were guarded by Roman soldiers so that no one could steal them. Mourning was also forbidden. People who wept in public over the death of an executed person were themselves executed. Tacitus reports concerning the mass executions under Tiberius: "Neither relatives nor friends were permitted to come close, to lament, even to look at them for any length of time." Any conduct expressing a close relation to the one crucified could lead to being crucified oneself.

The attitude of the women is in keeping with this reality: they stand "afar off" trying to remain unrecognized and yet risking their lives. The fact that they were women did not guarantee safety, for women and children were crucified too. To go to the grave was dangerous also. The Romans feared that graves of executed enemies of the empire could become places of pilgrimage for like-minded persons and centers for conspiratory elements. (Similarly, during the struggle of black South Africans against apartheid, there were many prohibitions of obsequies and services at the graves of murdered black children and teenagers.)

Quite consciously, Mary Magdalene and the other women choose to be witnesses, however cautiously. If they had been seen by informers on

Easter morning, it might have cost them their lives. The male disciples were therefore still hiding in Jerusalem at the time of the visit to the grave with the ointment. Fear held faith captive. The women were unable, thus, to follow the order of the "young man" to gather together the followers of Jesus who had been dispersed by the crucifixion. "They said nothing to anyone, for they were afraid" (Mark 16:8).

Mary Magdalene embodies the fear and the mourning of the whole community. She is more courageous than the men; she looks for Jesus outside at the grave, a public place avoided by the men. Her tears, often interpreted by biblical exegetes as mere sentimentality, are her most profound self-expression. The angels at the grave and even the risen Christ ask her, "Woman, why are you weeping?" (John 20:13, 15). Her tears bespeak the despair that all hope, all salvation was destroyed by Jesus' death. If God abandoned him and left him to the indifferent night of a universe without justice or peace, then the hope of the downtrodden to ever live free, fed, and without demons had died. According to the Gospel of John, Mary Magdalene recognizes Jesus only when he calls her by her name. She replies "'Rabbouni!' (which means Teacher)" (John 20:16). Jesus does not grant her wish to touch him and thereby to gain new strength. One is not supposed to touch the risen Lord. He touches people through the Holy Spirit, which he breathes into them (John 20:22). And he orders Mary Magdalene to tell the timid men what she as a witness has seen.

The disciples are still sitting in fear behind closed doors. They are servants of death. Mary Magdalene goes to them so that they may participate too. Resurrection is the sign of a power that changes life and breaks its subservience to and cooperation with death. The resurrection has need of witnesses, for it does not function here for the sake of Jesus' return to his Father, but for the sake of liberation of all people from fear and submission to the powers of death. One does not ask those without tears, "Why are you weeping?"

Above: Salvador Dali (1904–1989) shows mourning Mary Magdalene at the base of the cross, with plaintively raised hands.

Opposite: In his painting entitled Calvary, *Jacob Cornelisz van Oostsanen (ca. 1470–1533) shows Mary Magdalene kneeling in a gorgeous gown at the foot of the cross. Opposite her kneels Veronica with her veil, which has retained the imprint of Jesus' face.*

Page 143: In the foreground, Mary Magdalene kneels before the cross. With outstretched arms she gazes upon the crucified man, offering all her love. Her back, as well as the abundance of her curled hair, is turned away from the viewer. Detail from a crucifixion painting by Giovanni Bellini (ca. 1430–1516). Museo Civico, Pesaro

Above: Rembrandt van Rijn(1606–1669) had
already painted Christ Appears to Mary Magdalene
in 1638 but was again inspired by the subject in
1651, as shown here. The body of the risen Lord,
before whom Mary Magdalene drops to her knees,
is filled with light, illustrating Rembrandt's
concept of light conquering darkness.
Herzog-Anton-Ulrich-Museum, Braunschweig

Opposite: On Easter morning Jesus Christ
appears to Mary Magdalene who at first seems
stunned and recoils from what she takes to be
an apparition. Painting by Frederigo Baroccio
(ca. 1526/35–1612), a painter mostly active
in Urbino.
Galleria Corsini, Rome

Ancient and medieval sources

Joe H. Kirchberger

The Mary Magdalene described in the Gospels has undergone an amazing change in the course of centuries. Three of the four Gospels mention that she was present at the crucifixion (the exception being Luke). All four confirm her as a witness of the resurrection, noting even that Christ appeared to her first. It is further recorded that Christ freed her of "seven demons" (or devils). But nowhere is she called a sinner, for being cured by Christ cannot be interpreted as a remission of sins. Yet in the course of time she has become the embodiment of the repentant sinner, for in later versions she was merged with the "sinful woman" who anoints Jesus in the Gospel of Luke. She also came to be equated with Mary, the sister of Martha and Lazarus, as time went on.

This second phenomenon may be attributed in part to the fact that there are so many women called Mary in the New Testament. Aside from the mother of Christ and Lazarus's sister there are mentioned Mary, mother of the apostle James the Younger (the Less) and wife of Cleopas (possibly identical with the mother of the sons of Zebedee, who may have been the sister or half sister of the mother of Christ). Finally, there is Mary, "the mother of John whose surname was Mark" (Acts 12:12). Mary of Egypt, who is not a biblical but quite likely a historical personality who is said to have lived a life of sin in Alexandria before repenting and retreating for forty-seven years to the Syrian Desert, also contributes to the confusion.

MARY IS CALLED Magdalene after Magdala, a village probably identical with today's Majdol on the west shore of the Lake of Gennesaret. Since she is one of the main witnesses of Christ's rising from the dead, it seems peculiar that Paul does not count her as a witness in Corinthians 15. The enemies of the Christians even cited her as a counterwitness as she was regarded as "possessed," for instance by the Greek philosopher Celsus, whose *Logos Alethes* (Word of truth) was refuted in detail by the prominent Greek father of the church, Origin (186–254). Still, the earlier fathers distinguish her clearly from Luke's "sinner." Tatian, the *Heliand* (also around 830), and Otfried's *Liber Evangeliorum* (868) repeat the biblical story of her meeting Christ after his resurrection. But with the Magdalene homilies of Pope Gregory the Great (ca. 540–604), Magdalene begins to share features not only with the "sinner" but also with Mary of Egypt and the Samaritan woman of John 4 who was converted by Christ when she met him at the Sychar well. In the *Life of Jesus* of Ava, the first German woman poet known by name who probably died at the Melk monastery in Lower Austria in 1127, all biblical material is treated in the light of mankind's redemption. Mary Magdalene is still distinguished clearly from Martha's sister. For Martha's sister is an introvert who would hardly have stood at the cross and exposed herself to the mockery of Pharisees and soldiers, while Magdalene is a brave and extroverted woman. But Odo von Cluny, who died in 942, follows Gregory's interpretations and sees already in Magdalene's being "possessed" the consequences of her sinful life. Konrad, a priest who lived near Lake Geneva around 1170 and of whose German sermons 114 are preserved, proceeds in a similar way. His theological counterpart is the popular Franciscan preacher Berthold von Regensburg (1210–1272), a follower of the Franciscan prophet Joachim of Floris, who announced an "Age of the Spirit" for 1260. Together with Albertus Magnus he was summoned by Pope Urban VI to deliver sermons against the Waldensians, who were regarded as heretics. No less than 258 of his sermons have been preserved. Yet he, too, follows the tradition of Gregory and Odo, as does the French Dominican Vincent of Beauvais in his collection of Bible stories.

The Middle Ages saw in Peter, Paul, and Mary the three great penitents: Peter because he denied his Lord, Paul because he persecuted the Christians before his conversion, Mary Magdalene because she had led a life of sin.

A COMPLETELY NEW MOTIF is added by the *Legenda Aurea* (ca. 1270) and thereafter in the poem *Der saelden hort* (1298). They make Magdalene the forsaken bride of the "beloved"

Opposite Mary Magdalene, presented as a wealthy, fashionably coiffured young woman. Unpainted wooden sculpture from Brabant, around 1500. Musée Cluny, Paris

At the church of Aix, Mary Magdalene addresses the congregation from the pulpit. By an unknown Swiss artist, early sixteenth century. Fürstlich-Fürstenbergische Sammlungen, Donaueschingen

disciple John, who devoted his life completely to service of Christ.

Since the ninth century, July 22 has been the official feast day for Mary Magdalene, and since then about 1,100 hymns have been written in her honor. Two rhymed poems about her come from Lower Austria, one by the Cistercian Christian von Lilienfeld (before 1330), the other by the Carthusian monk Konrad von Gaming (around 1350). Dante does not mention her in his *Divine Comedy*, but she does appear in his *Convivio* (The banquet), written in exile around 1305 when he develops his philosophical and literary principles.

Most of the medieval *Lamentations of Mary Magdalene* are utterances of repentance, but some also express compassion and love. The latter can be traced back to Gregory the Great. Here Mary is represented as the mourning bride searching for her beloved, thus linking the biblical *Noli me tangere* (Touch me not, John 20:17 KJV) with the Song of Solomon (Song of Songs) of the Old Testament. The same connection is made by the Austrian epic poet Heinrich von Neustadt (1330). Magdalene was also regarded as liberator of captives, as in the Low German poem *Van sante Maria Magdalena*, around 1450. Other medieval stories identify her with the Samaritan penitent who met Jesus at the well, or confuse her with Mary of Egypt. A special Magdalene cult developed at Vézelay in the heartland of France where construction of the great St. Madeleine Church was begun in 1096. Here the penitent life of Mary of Egypt was transferred to Magdalene and her companion Maximinus. An old talmudic tradition has a different story: Magdalene, as "Miriam," is the bride of Rabbi Papos ben Jehuda. Konrad, around 1170, also hints at that connection.

THE MOST BEAUTIFUL LEGENDS originate in southern France where Magdalene is merged with Martha's sister. It is said that she started preaching at Marseilles, initially without success. This changed when she performed a miracle. She raised from the dead a baby whose mother had died in childbirth. The child's father was on a trip to Jerusalem where he sought reassurance that Magdalene had preached the truth. In Jerusalem Peter showed him all the sacred places and instructed him for two years. When he finally returned to Marseilles, his child, whom he had left dead on the mother's breast, was alive and well, and ran along the shore collecting stones and shells. Then, when he lifted the cloth from his wife's body, she opened her eyes and stretched out her arms for him. After this miracle many believed and were baptized.

The *Legenda Aurea* tells the story somewhat differently: The governor of the province of Marseilles, Peregrinus, was ready to become a Christian if Mary Magdalene would pray for him to have a child. She did so, and his wife soon conceived. He and his pregnant wife embarked on a journey to meet Peter. But the woman died in childbirth and was left behind on a small island with the child still alive. Now Peregrinus lamented: "Why did you advise me to go on this journey? Do not let the child perish!" Peter consoled him: "Do not despair, for your wife is resting and the little child with her!" Peregrinus spent two years in the Holy Land and on the way back arrived at the small island. His little boy was playing at the shore. But when he saw Peregrinus, he fled to his dead mother, as he had never seen a man. Peregrinus found him drinking from his mother's breast and said, "Oh, if she were alive and would return home with me!" at which point she woke up. In her spirit she had participated in the whole journey, holding on to Magdalene's hand, and knew all about it. The three then returned to Marseilles overjoyed, recounted the whole story to Magdalene, and were baptized by Maximinus.

The *Legenda Aurea* adds that Magdalene is able to free captives out of a debtor's prison; sailors invoke her as a saint of the sea, and she brings light to those lost in the dark. It is said that a man recorded all his sins on a piece of paper and put it under the cloth of Magdalene's altar, thus winning the intercession of the saint and forgiveness of his sins. The *Legenda* also speaks of a soldier who visited Magdalene's grave every few years. When he was killed in battle, his parents complained that Mary Magdalene had let him die without confession. Thereupon the dead man rose, asked for a priest, confessed, received the viaticum, and passed away in peace. After all these miracles, Magdalene is said to have returned to the desert and lived there as a hermit for thirty years. In her later years she had visions. Every day angels lifted her up so she could hear the heavenly harmonies and could see how repentant sinners are respected. One day a hermit saw her being carried by singing angels and proclaimed it in the city of Marseilles.

In 1279, her own and Lazarus's earthly remains were discovered near Toulon. Count Eberhard of Provence built a church at the spot. When later he was taken captive by the king of Aragon, he was reportedly freed by Mary Magdalene, and her reputation in southern France rose even higher.

The rose is one of her emblems. In most presentations she herself is clad in violet, the color of repentance and expiation. Usually she is shown

NE DESP
ETIS.
UOS QUI
PECCARE
SOLETIS.
EXEMPLO
OB. MEO.
UOS REPA
RATE.DE
O

Opposite: In this icon-style representation by an Italian painter of the thirteenth century, Mary Magdalene stands frontally before the beholder with a banderole in her hand. It reads: "Do not despair if you have sinned. Follow my example and make your peace with God!" On the eight small scenes around Mary Magdalene the most important stages of her life are pictured. Galleria dell'Accademia, Florence

First row:
Left: Mary Magdalene bathes Jesus' feet in tears, dries them with her hair, and pours precious perfume over them.
Right: Here she is a witness when Jesus orders Lazarus, who had been dead in his grave for three days, to return to life. The legend often confuses Mary Magdalene with Mary of Bethany, sister of Lazarus and Martha.

Second row:
Left: Mary Magdalene rejoices when she sees Jesus actually standing in front of her on Easter morning. She wants to embrace the beloved Master, but Jesus says: "Noli me tangere!" (Do not touch me).
Right: Mary Magdalene preaching at the church of Aix where she landed after she and her companions were washed ashore at Marseilles in a rudderless boat.

Third row:
Left: While praying, Mary Magdalene is lifted by angels and hovers aloft during her contemplation.
Right: While living the life of a penitent in the desert, Mary Magdalene is fed by an angel.

Fourth row:
Left: Maximinus hands the holy sacrament to Mary Magdalene.
Right: Mary Magdalene is buried at Aix. After Aix's destruction her relics were brought to Vézelay.

Right: Mary Magdalene is often confused with the Egyptian penitent Mary, as in this wooden statuette by Gregor Erhart, from approximately 1500, showing La belle Allemande nude, covered only by her long hair.
Musée du Louvre, Paris

with long hair, holding a small box with ointments, sometimes also with a flaming heart. The word "maudlin" (tearful, overly sentimental) is derived from Magdalene, meaning originally "shedding tears of repentance."

IN SUM, IT CAN BE SAID that in the Middle Ages Mary Magdalene, as one of the main witnesses of the crucifixion and the resurrection, illustrated that sinful mankind could be redeemed. But she also embodied converted paganism and the *ecclesia* (church), as in Gottschalk von Limburg's *Laus tibi, Christe* (Praise to thee, Christ) of the eleventh century and in Hermann von Reichenau around the same time. For the French of the High Middle Ages she is the sinner par excellence, as with Marbode in his *Peccatrix quondam femina* (There once was a sinful woman), and with Gottfried von Vendôme. A little later, under the influence of mysticism, she turned into the image of the soul searching for Jesus. She is portrayed as such in the hymn "*Lauda, mater ecclesiae*" by Alan of Lille, in several songs of Peter the Venerable, and also in a hymn for the blessed sinner, written by the then very famous teacher of theology and philosophy

Abelard (1079–1142), whose tragic love for his pupil Heloise has been taken up in literature time and time again. In the later Middle Ages the image of Magdalene as the penitent sinner predominates again, as in one of the many versions of a popular folk song from the sixteenth century in which she repents for a long time but is not redeemed because she has looked at her hands "in a non-humble way," and therefore must repent for another seven years. An English folk song of about the same period shows her as a Samaritan courtesan who meets Jesus at the well of Sychar. In another late medieval legend, she accompanies John to Ephesus and is buried there, while earlier reports describe the transfer of her relics from Provence to Burgundy. The identification with the Samaritan woman at the well is also found in a medieval German folk song: "*Magdalena hin zur Quelle geht*" (Magdalene is going to the well).

In the passion plays of the late Middle Ages there are frequently long Magdalene scenes that show for the first time her worldly life as a sinner.

A popular motif in representations of Mary Magdalene is her mystical elevation while she engages in ecstatic prayer.

Opposite: painting by Paolo Veronese (1528–1588).
Museo del Prado, Madrid

Right: painting by José Antolinez (1635–1675), a master of the Spanish high baroque.
Museo del Prado, Madrid

Bibliography

Ascher, Mary: *Twelve Women of the Old Testament.* New York, 1963.

Barash, Asher: *Arabic Folk Tales.* Masada, 1969.

Boccaccio, Giovanni: *De claris mulieribus* (ca. 1365). German edition. Tübingen, 1895.

Boyajian, Z. C.: *Armenian Legends and Poems.* London, 1916.

Carmody, Denise Lardner: *Biblical Women.* New York, 1988.

Chalier, Catherine: *Les matriarches.* Paris, 1985.

Deen, Ed.: *All the Women of the Bible.* New York, 1955.

Eger, Paul: *Adam, Eva und die Schlange.* Munich, 1920.

Every, George: *Christian Mythology.* London, New York, n.d.

Faulhaber, Michael: *Charakterbilder der biblischen Frauenwelt.* 1935–58.

Flavius Josephus: *Jewish Antiquities* (German trans. H. Clementz). Wiesbaden, 1990.

Frenzel, Elizabeth: *Stoffe der Weltliteratur.* Stuttgart, 1983.

Frye, Northrop: *Words with Power.* New York, 1990.

Gaer, Joseph: *The Lore of the Old Testament.* Boston, 1951.

Gaer, Joseph: *The Lore of the New Testament.* Boston, 1952.

Gesta Romanorum (medieval collection of ancient legends), fourteenth century, German ed. Leipzig, 1905.

Ginzburg, Louis: *Legends of the Jews.* 7 vols., Philadelphia, 1956.

Goodspeed, Edgar J.: *Strange New Gospels,* Freeport, N.Y., 1971.

Gravelaine, Jovelle de: *Le Retour de Lilith.* Paris, 1985.

Guenter, Heinrich: *Psychology of Legend.* Freiburg, 1949.

Hackwood, Fred W.: *Christ Lore.* London, 1902.

Hahn, Friedrich: *Bibel und moderne Literatur.* Stuttgart, 1968.

Hatz, Mechthild: *Frauengestalten des Alten Testaments.* Heidelberg, 1972.

Kahana, S. Z.: *Legends of Israel.* 1987.

Kappstein, Theodor: *Bibel und Sage.* Berlin, 1913.

Karssen, Gien: *Frauen der Bibel* (trans. L. Friedemann).

Koltuv, Barbara: *The Book of Lilith.* York Beach, 1986.

Koran, The (trans. Laz. Goldschmidt). Berlin, 1956.

Lafargue, Paul: *The Myth of Adam and Eve.* Chicago, 1928.

Liptzin, Sol: *Biblical Themes in World Literature.* Hoboken, N.J., 1985.

McKenzie: *Dictionary of the Bible.*

Modersohn, Ernst: *Die Frauen des Neuen Testaments.* Stuttgart, 1989.

Philo Judaeus. *Works.* Loeb Libr. 1929–1942.

Rossetti, Christina: *Poems.* Boston, 1866.

Sachs, Hans: *Werke.* 1870–1908. Ed. K. Kinzel. Halle, 1905.

Shaw, George Bernard: *Back to Methuselah* (play). London, 1947.

Singer, Isaac: *The Wicked City.* New York, 1972.

Smitt, F. A.: *Stoff- und Motivgeschichte der deutschen Literatur.* Berlin, 1976.

Stadler, J. E. und Heim, J.: *Vollständiges Heiligen-Lexikon.* Augsburg, 1855–57.

Stowe, Harriet Elizabeth Beecher: *Women in Sacred History.* New York, 1873.

Talmud, Worte des, ed. Rabbi Goldstein. Tübingen, 1963.

Toynbee, Paget J.: *A Dictionary of Proper Names of Dante.* Oxford, 1914.

Urbanek, Gisela: *Die Gestalt König Davids.* Vienna, 1964.

Väterbuch, Das (Vitae Patrum) (collection of legends). Leipzig, 1914. Autour de 1280.

Voragine, Jacobus de: *Der Heiligen Leben und Leiden* (The golden legend). 2 vols., Leipzig, 1913.

Weil, G.: *Biblical Legends of the Mussulmans.* New York, 1846.

Work, E. W.: *The Bible in English Literature.* New York, 1917.

Zweig, Arnold: *Abigail und Nabal* (tragedy). Leipzig, 1913.

Literary Sources

Note to the Dorothee Soelle texts:
For the description of biblical women, I have used Karin Walter, ed., *Zwischen Ohnmacht and Befreiung. Biblische Frauengestalten*. Freiburg, Basel, Vienna: Herder Frauenforum, 1988.

Unless otherwise noted, Scripture quotations are from the New Revised Standard Version of the Bible, Copyright © 1989 by the Division of Christian Education of the National Council of the Churches of Christ in the U.S.A., and used by permission.

Photo Credits
a = above; b = below

Arte Fotografia, Rome: 147
Beyer Constantin, Munich: 83
Biblioteca Apostolica Vaticana, Vatican: 31, 78
Boyer Patrick, Montlouis sur Loire: 44
Boymans-van-Beuningen Museum, Rotterdam: 132/133
British Library, London: 12, 33, 57, 81 b
Burgerbibliothek, Bern: 34
County Museum of Art, Los Angeles: 130
EMB-Archiv, Adligenswil: all not mentioned pictures
Giraudon, Paris: 4 (4), 5 (10), 55, 73, 122, 123, 126/127, 128, 135
Goerlipp Georg, Donaueschingen: 150
Herzog-Anton-Ulrich-Museum, Braunschweig: 146
Kunsthistorisches Museum, Vienna: 32, 92
La Fotocamera, Genoa: 38/39
MAS Ampliaciones y Reproducciones, Barcelona: 110
Metropolitan Museum, New York: 16/17, 27
Münsterbauverein, Freiburg i.Br.: 37
Musée des Beaux Arts, Tours: 44
Museo del Prado, Madrid: 7, 77, 90/91, 137, 154, 155
Museo San Rocco, Venice: 20
National Gallery of Canada, Ottawa: 102
National Museum, Budapest: 111 a
Nippon Television Network Corporation, Tokyo: 11, 22/23, 67, 114/115
Pinacoteca Nazionale, Bologna: 104/105
Reiss Ferdinand, Vorau: 111 b
Réunion des Musées Nationaux, Paris: 5 (5, 7, 11), 8, 41, 49, 60/61, 65, 69, 86, 101, 106 a, 149, 153
Rijksmuseum Stichting, Amsterdam: 140/141, 145
Rivaux Jean-Pierre, Buxerolles: 51
Sereni Michele Alberto, Pesaro: 143
Staatsgalerie, Stuttgart: 84
Staats- und Universitätsbibliothek, Hamburg: 81 a, 96, 97
Tate Gallery, London: 19, 25, 28, 138/139
Topkapi-Serail-Museum, Istanbul: 17
Victoria and Albert Museum, London: 63
Wallraf-Richartz-Museum, Cologne: 140

Index